Because We Have Good News

Because We Have Good News

Wallace E. Fisher

Nashville   Abingdon Press   New York

Library of Congress Cataloging in Publication Data

FISHER, WALLACE E. Because we have good news. Includes
bibliographical references. 1. Evangelistic work. I. Title.
BV3790.F543   269'.2   73-12233

ISBN 0-687-02532-X

MANUFACTURED BY THE PARTHENON PRESS AT
NASHVILLE, TENNESSEE, UNITED STATES OF AMERICA

To All Christophers:
For Evangelism Is Cross-Bearing

Acknowledgments

In a concise summary of this sort, it is not possible to list all the sources I have used, or to acknowledge fully my debt to Christian and secular writers who have lighted my path, or to express adequately my gratitude to lay and clerical colleagues who have helped me. But the dedication, occasional footnotes, and following paragraph make a stab at it.

My secretary, Mrs. Arline S. Fellenbaum, deserves thanks for preparing the manuscript; and Mrs. Judy Armstrong and Mrs. Cynthia Henry, office secretaries, for helping. Clyde E. Brown, Jr., R. Ray Evelan, and Larry L. Lehman, associates at Trinity Church; Gabriel Fackre, Donald R. Heiges, Jack R. Hoffman (a former associate on Trinity's Staff), Roger Lovett, and Harald Sigmar, ministerial colleagues in Newton Centre, Massachusetts; Gettysburg, Pennsylvania; Hanover, Pennsylvania; Lexington, Kentucky; and Yakima, Washington; and Robert P. Desch, Melvin J. Evans, and Ann H. Musselman, lay evangelists in Trinity, have read the manuscript, offering valuable comments. Our son, Mark, Chapel Hill, North Carolina, has shortened the text and kept the language down-to-earth. My wife, Margaret Elizabeth, knows better than anyone my debt to her.

Lancaster, Pennsylvania   WALLACE E. FISHER

Preface

Voltaire complained that "all books are too long." Most Americans, deluged by words and bombarded by books, would agree. This study book is concise and concrete. It aims to encourage and equip laymen to evangelize person-to-person.

During 1973, one hundred and forty Protestant denominations and sects, liberal and conservative—and in some areas Catholic churches—labored unevenly to revitalize and/or deepen commitment to the Christian work of personal evangelism at the grass roots. Each Protestant denomination and sect, and Catholic church—indeed, every participating congregation—was free to proceed as it determined. Key 73, as the ecumenical venture was called, was an emphasis rather than a program. Theodore Raedeke, former director of evangelism in the Lutheran Church–Missouri Synod, directed the ecumenical venture. Billy Graham was its most generous and best-known supporter.[1]

Because of this conservative cast, and other factors, several main-line Protestant denominations declined to participate. A solid bloc of participants expressed concern that the nationwide emphasis on person-to-person evangelism would turn into a retreat from God's firm claim on his church to serve in the world. Most agreed, however, that this ecumenical call to the churches to focus on shar-

---

[1] Dr. Graham urges those who are "converted" at his mass meetings to identify with a local church.

ing the gospel with persons in one's own community could be a wholesome venture. In the Lutheran Church in America, for example, Raymond May, director of the Key 73 emphasis, declared readily that the primary focus was on reaching persons outside the congregation (a proper Christian task); but he stated firmly that "a concern for justice, peace, and community renewal is also an integral part of witnessing to the power and purpose of the gospel." Whether the 1973 nationwide ecumenical emphasis on evangelism will generate a "numbers game" (as in the 1950s), blunt the church's enlarged concern for persons in society, provide a sanctuary for escapists from the world, or turn out to be confusion roughly organized, cannot be judged accurately for several years. But all participants can be certain now that if *their* evangelistic work does not root in the gospel, if it fails to communicate the Good News, they will have another activistic foray to absorb. In spite of these obvious risks, thousands of clergy and the congregations they serve set out hopefully in 1973 to revitalize or sharpen their evangelistic endeavors. In many quarters of main-line Protestantism, that task was overdue. During the preceding decade, some of these churches had become preoccupied with demonstrating their concern to make social structures more humane. Now, without surrendering that objective, they set out to persuade persons to accept Christ and serve him through his church.

The basic objective in person-to-person evangelism is to present Christ *as he is* so that persons *as they are* will decide for or against him *and his church.* Expectantly then, the outcome is problematical in each evangelistic encounter. Andrew evangelized Peter; he responded affirmatively. Paul presented the Christian cause to Herod Agrippa; the King deferred his decision, suggesting that Paul "come at a more convenient season." Jesus advised the Rich Young Ruler to sell his possessions and join his itinerant ministry; the young man, sorrowing, refused. Paul preached Christ in Ephesus; he was run out of town. Each of those responses reflect *effective* Christian witness. Some people say yes, others procrastinate; some say no, others become hostile.

This book is on this order. Chapter 1 defines evangelistic work—its dynamic, content, and varied styles. Chapter 2 examines some common reasons people give for declining to unite with a particular congregation. Chapter 3 examines the crucial need for integrity in the church's care of persons. Chapter 4 attempts a panoramic view of church and society in America in the 1970s. Chapter 5 enumerates some practical suggestions for evangelizing.

The book can be used by church members for individual study. It will be more useful, however, if it is studied and discussed in group sessions—church councilmen, evangelists-in-training, and congregation-wide cottage meetings. Each of the chapters can be used for single sessions, or four sessions can be scheduled, omitting chapter 5. Another alternative is to schedule three sessions, by combining chapters 2 and 3, and omitting chapter 5. The book can also be shared profitably with prospective members if their attention is called to chapters 1-3. However it is used—and each congregation will decide that for itself—one hopes that Protestant and Catholic clergy will find it useful in motivating and equipping laymen to do "the greatest work in the world." The title of the book—*Because We Have Good News*—is integral to the book's content. That is the heart of Christian evangelism. Consequently, it is the only proper theme for a study of evangelism.

The material in the book has been presented in its several parts at the Southern Baptist Theological Seminary, Louisville, Kentucky; the Annual Pastors' Convocation, Lutheran Theological Seminary, Chicago, Illinois; the Annual Seminary Week, Gettysburg Theological Seminary, Gettysburg, Pennsylvania; the Annual Pastors' Institute, Princeton Theological Seminary; the Annual Pastors' Convocation, Andover-Newton Theological Seminary; the Nevada-California District, Lutheran Church–Missouri Synod, San Francisco; a United Methodist Conference on Continuing Education for Pastors, Fort Wayne, Indiana; and the Chaplains Corps, the United States Marine Base, Camp Lejeune, North Carolina. Two chapters were prepared originally for an interdenominational Key 73 dialogical workshop at Myrtle Beach, South Carolina.

Trinity Church, Lancaster, Pennsylvania, has been the testing ground for the material presented here—and so much more. Trinity's members tried it, did not like some of it at first, yet found most of it palatable, sustaining, enriching. My gratitude to this gallant-hearted congregation is beyond expression. I thank God for our life together in Christ during these twenty-one exciting years.

Contents

I
The Evangelist
His Person and His Credentials

The goal of Christian ministry is to bring wholeness to the human spirit. If the human spirit is viewed realistically as an embodied spirit and treated so, and if embodied spirits are motivated and encouraged to serve persons and to fashion the just society for the sake of the kingdom of God, then everything that a congregation says and does to demonstrate God's reconciling deed in Christ is evangelism. Every sermon, worship service, counseling session, study class, dialogue group, pastoral visit, hospital visit, prospective member call, social involvement, youth program, and ecumenical venture which presents or orients to Christ *as he is,* is evangelistic work.

Essentially, Christian evangelism is the sharing of the Good News so that persons in their freedom are persuaded to say "yes" or "no" to Christ and his church. This sharing employs various emphases, forms, and styles. Luther's style of evangelism was firmly tied to his incarnational theology. John Wesley developed a style inseparable from his view of liturgy, the sacraments, revivalistic preaching, and social concerns. William Temple refused to separate evangelism from social action. Dietrich Bonhoeffer merged evangelism with political action. The dean of evangelists, Paul, linked his experience of Christ with his disciplined doing of God's will *in the world*. That is how he came to be shipwrecked, beaten, imprisoned, martyred. He was witnessing to Christ *in the world*. Evangelism is an integral part of the gospel itself. Any congregation that neglects it ceases to be the church of Jesus Christ.

Christian evangelism, personal and corporate, persuades some persons to accept Christ; it alienates others. That is because the heart of evangelism is the Word of God. His Word is a two-edged sword: one edge cuts, the other heals. But many churches emasculate the Word of the Lord. They proclaim a crossless Christ to a world that is being crucified on a Christless cross. They cheapen Christ's promises by muting his demands. They obscure the Incarnation by ignoring or minimizing the clamorous claims of their historical situation. A church that does not share the *whole* Word *in* the world is unfaithful to its Lord. Consequently, it is, as Paul Tillich observed three decades ago, a perishing community in a perishing culture.

It is an awesome experience to fall into the hands of a gracious God. The human ego is shattered; then it is refashioned. When one accepts Christ, the old creature becomes new, but even so he remains a creature. But this rebirth of the spirit is a radical experience. Jesus cautioned eager recruits to count the cost of discipleship before they committed themselves to him. He admonished his fellow-evangelists against casting pearls before swine. His parable of the soils is crystal clear in defining the successes and the failures inherent in Christian evangelism. And there on Calvary, the Chief Evangelist won one thief to his way of life; but he lost the other. Activistic churchmen who mount church membership drives need to be reminded that Jesus did not adjust God's purposes to suit those who wanted the kingdom on their terms. The Christian God desires committed friends, not casual acquaintances. He wants sons, not slaves. And he expects "his people" to promote justice and mercy among all people. God, honoring man's freedom, wants persons to decide *for* or *against* him. And what God wants is the proper goal of evangelism if it is to be *Christian*.

Although some churchmen who were involved in Key 73 expressed concern lest the church replay the numbers game of the 1950s, others were more concerned that segments of the church would take up person-to-person evangelism to escape the ambiguous, frustrating, yet necessary personal and congregational involvements with the socioeconomic and political realities of our day. Every authentic Christian evangelist knows that he cannot separate the ego-shattering experience of the Damascus Road from the risk-taking ministry of the Jericho Road.

Evangelistic work must be carried on primarily by the laity. This should be obvious to "Christians." The sixteenth-century Reformers recovered that biblical concept of the priesthood of believers. Unfortunately, the American Protestant church—especially in the nineteenth and twentieth centuries—perverted that concept to read that each member in every congregation is free to think, say, and do what pleases him, his family, and/or his peer group. The biblical concept of the priesthood of all believers rests on the assumption that each church member, having accepted the Lordship of Christ, is constrained to discern and do God's will.[1] Christ is the only authority

---

[1] See Wallace E. Fisher, *Preface to Parish Renewal* (Nashville: Abingdon Press, 1968), chapter 2, "By Whose Authority?" This paperback for *laymen* examines, in chapter 2, the relation-

who can bring order out of chaos; who can turn diversity
into unity. Luther observed that while all members of the
Christian church are priests, they are not all clergymen.
He meant that (a) Christian ministry is a function (an
office) not an order; (b) the professional exercise of
ministry must be in the hands of persons trained and
approved by the church; and (c) lay members are called
to be teachers, healers, and *evangelists*. Christian evangelistic work (viewed biblically and theologically), like
the care and nurture of church members, is a *primary*
work of the whole congregation.

Adolph Harnack, describing evangelism in the early
church, wrote that "the most numerous and successful
missionaries of the Christian religion were not the regular
teachers but the Christians themselves, by dint of their
loyalty and courage." Justin Martyr, an early defender of
the Faith, committed himself to Christ during a person-to-
person conversation with an elderly Christian gentleman
as the two men walked along the Mediterranean seaside.
In the fourth century, Jerome stated that "baptism is the
ordination of the laity." Each baptized member, he said,
is ordained to evangelize. In the thirteenth century,
Thomas Aquinas taught that every church member "is
given power and responsibility, not only to perfect his
own salvation, but also, by sharing in the priesthood of
Christ, to act as his apostle in the salvation of the world."
A quarter of a century ago the Church of England admonished its laity that "confirmation, from earliest times,

---

ship between the Bible and the Word of God. Other chapters,
especially chapters 4 and 5, "The Significance of Leadership" and
"Creative Conflict," are relevant for the evangelizing congregation.

has been considered the ordination of the laity, when they are commissioned and empowered to exercise their apostleship of evangelism." The laity in the Wesleyan Revival reshaped the manners and morals of the eighteenth-century English proletariat. In every generation, evangelistic work depends on the laity. The late D. T. Niles, of Ceylon, had this in mind when he defined evangelism simply as "following Christ."

But church members, lay and ordained, are disposed to give up on evangelistic work. They are inclined to take up less frustrating and less demanding tasks in the congregation's care of persons. Church members must be motivated and recalled periodically, therefore, to the demanding work of evangelism. That is a gut reason why churchmen got involved in Key 73. Certainly, no mature Christian took seriously that slogan about winning North America for Christ! That was propaganda, pure and simple. Unrealistic and unbiblical, it smacked of an earlier brand of "Christian" imperialism which looked arrogantly on all non-Christians (Jews, agnostics, Buddhists, Hindus, humanists, atheists) as inferior people; and that is foreign to the spirit of Christ.

On the other hand, a majority of persons, participants in Key 73, set out to persuade church members to take up the hard work of person-to-person evangelism which the church had attempted casually in the 1950s, and had worked at fitfully in the turbulent 1960s. They encouraged their fellow-Christians to discover in worship, Bible study, and firsthand experience that (a) evangelistic work depends on the laity, (b) the dynamic for evangelism roots in one's commitment to Christ, (c) the content of

evangelism is the Word of God, and (d) the place where
evangelistic work is done is *in the world*.

But personal commitment to Christ is not enough
to guarantee effective Christian evangelism. The evangelist
must also understand the gospel (be able to give a reason
for his commitment). Neither are commitment to Christ
and a solid understanding of the gospel enough. The
evangelist must also understand the cultural situation in
which he seeks to make his witness. Otherwise, his testimony will be blunted, aborted, ignored. The Christian
evangelist must recognize that he lives in the land of the
Philistines, speaks the language of the Philistines, marries
into the families of the Philistines, and works side by side
with the Philistines, even though he does not worship the
gods of the Philistines. For the effectivenss of his person-
to-person witness, granted his personal commitment to
Christ and understanding of the gospel, depends on his
competence to understand the Philistines, speak their
language, identify their gods, appreciate their *human*
needs, and accept them as *persons*. The unchurched are
not objects to be manipulated for the sake of an institution; they are persons to be loved, accepted, served, and
persuaded to accept Christ—if their wills agree.

Contemporary Christian evangelists have the arduous
and ambiguous task of communicating the gospel to (a)
those whom Frederich Schleiermacher called its "cultured
despisers"; (b) those whom Kierkegaard claimed "had
done away with Christianity without being aware of it";
(c) those who have no knowledge of the Christian God
and little sense of self-identity; (d) those who have lost
all hope in all contemporary institutions, especially the

church; (e) those who are desperately lonely; (f) those who are alienated from self and society.

The disposition in some conservative church circles to encourage laymen simply to tell "the old, old story" limits the range and power of the church's witness to Christ. Equally, the casual attitude in confessional churches to regard the pulpit ("professional" preachers) and the church school (a little band of lay teachers— mostly female) as being adequate to expand the kingdom of God aborts *personal* evangelism. Person-to-person evangelism, if it is to be effective, requires the laity to be committed to Christ and to be cultural realists as well as loyalists to Christ's church.

Jesus was a realist about his culture and about persons in that culture. He knew that insecure religious leaders and devious political leaders would bring about his humiliation and death. He called the wily Herod "that fox." He predicted the defection of his disciples under pressure. He warned that Jerusalem would be leveled by the Romans as a security measure. He declined to discuss his mission with Pilate. Paul, too, was a cultural realist. He preached Christ crucified, but to do that effectively he borrowed freely from Judaism and Hellenism. The Apostle understood both cultures as well as he understood the Christian message. Actually, it was his commitment to Christ and his understanding of the gospel which enabled him to be so alert and curious in and open to *the world*.

Many twentieth-century Protestants wish that Luther had perceived more sharply the chaotic social-economic-political realities of sixteenth-century Europe. But in spite of that serious limitation, Luther—gustily at home in his provincial world—was an earthy man who loved his Katherine, his children, his beer, his rousing arguments with friend and foe, and his God. It was that wholesome *earthiness* that helped him to understand, formulate, and communicate incarnational theology better than anyone else since Paul.[2] Wesley associated day after day with the depressed proletariat of England; he knew firsthand how the socio-economic-political structures of eighteenth-century England dehumanized the proletariat. Dietrich Bonhoeffer was a hard-nosed political realist as well as a disciplined Christian believer. Christian witness requires faith in, knowledge of, and obedience to God *in his world*. After all, the world is the only place where Christians can witness. If *that* witness is not made, the church ceases to be the church of Jesus Christ.[3]

Since the difficulties encountered in witnessing to this generation root not only in our persons and our understanding of the gospel, but also in contemporary culture, it is necessary that lay evangelists be equipped to distinguish between appearance and reality in the world. The brief outline below can be expanded, implemented, and presented concretely for discussion by the pastor or a lay member.

[2] Any layman will profit from reading Roland Bainton's biography of Luther, *Here I Stand* (paperback ed.: Nashville: Abingdon Press, 1950).

[3] Rolf Hochuth, *The Deputy* (New York: Grove Press, 1964), charges that Pope Pius XII valued the institutional church above the welfare of the Jews living under Nazi domination, 1934-1945. Consider, too, the widespread worship of the Bible as an end rather than a means in some Protestant circles. Consider also the mechanical stewardship programs in many main-line Protestant churches aimed at getting a dollar; they are not distinguishable from secular appeals except for the "pious" language.

The successive and interrelated social critiques of Nietzsche, Marx, and Freud in the nineteenth century fell in the fertile soil of a deteriorating historical situation in the West. The Congress of Vienna (1815) stabilized the European states until 1914. Thereafter, World War I, an economic depression that shook the socio-economic-political foundations of the industrial nations, the rise of totalitarian states (Soviet Russia, Fascist Italy, Nazi Germany), World War II, the advent of nuclear weapons, the unprecedented surge in technology, Asia in ferment, Africa in revolt, Latin America seething—all this disheartened, and in some quarters overwhelmed, the institutional church first in Europe and then in America. These colossal dislocations, linked with the secularization of life inside the church in the West, made it appear that Carlyle's sweeping judgment—Christ has had his day—was being fulfilled and that Nietzsche's call for the revision of *all* values was valid. Valid or not, that revision (which got underway in America during the 1920s) was at full tide in the 1960s. Millions of people were convinced that "everythin' nailed down was comin' loose." But millions of others called it "liberation." Both segments of society provided a reading public large enough to make Joseph Fletcher's *Situation Ethics,* John Robinson's *Honest to God,* Vance Packard's *Sexual Wilderness,* and Harvey Cox's *Secular City* best sellers during the 1960s.

Unless the Christian evangelist is equipped to converse relevantly with people who are staggering under present shock and cowering before future shock, he will be ineffective. The evangelist, living in the world like everyone else, is constrained by the gospel to bring his maturing Christian insights to bear on persons, ideas, and sociopolitical structures so that men, nations, and races will know that the grace and power of the Christian God is at work among them. Otherwise, the church he represents is irrelevant in the world. Working steadily under these tough demands, the concerned evangelist discovers that there is a time to speak and a time to listen, a time to proclaim and a time to dialogue, a time to pray and a time to plan, a time to act and a time to wait.

It is understandable, therefore, that some churchmen consider that the task of the Christian evangelist is more difficult in 1974 than it was in the decade following World War II. *Quantitatively,* that judgment appears to be accurate. The social turbulence and theological confusion of the 1960s—the frustrations and defeats, the satisfactions and victories—sobered, chastened, disillusioned, and disheartened millions of American citizens. Consequently, these buffeted people are not eager, nor inclined presently, to join *any* organization. On the other hand, many people outside the church *are* interested in learning how to live meaningfully, how to be responsible mates and parents, how to overmatch loneliness, how to reshape the structures of an urban-technological society which dehumanize man and despoil nature, how to live creatively with present shock, and how to cope effectively with future shock.[4] *Qualitatively,* then, the cultural climate of the mid-1970s is more hospitable to *Christian* evangelism than was the climate of the 1950s.

I am not suggesting that the majority of Americans are concerned with the quality of life for themselves and others; they are not. My argument here is that the

[4] See Alvin Toffler's *Future Shock* (New York: Random House, 1970).

temper of mind among millions of Americans between 1953 and 1974 has changed, and that this change makes many Americans more open to the Christ of faith than to the Christ of culture. In 1974, thousands of churchmen know the difference between an efficient religious institution and a maturing Christian fellowship of concern; they yearn for the church to be a helping, serving, prodding, healing community in which the Christian's intimate experience of Christ motivates and enables him to serve God and man in the world. The 1970s offer a hospitable climate for *Christian* witness; in some respects the climate resembles that of the first Christian century.

Now, at this juncture in the discussion, we elect to substitute in the remainder of this chapter the noun *"witness"* for the noun "evangelist." We judge that this word is a sound vehicle for our teaching purposes. Also, a change in words may be refreshing after the overexposure to "evangelism" in 1973! Jesus himself said: "You shall be my *witnesses* in Jerusalem and in all Judea and Samaria and to the end of the earth." (Acts 1:8 RSV.)

Simply, a witness is one who sees a particular event and speaks about what he has observed. Two cars collide at an intersection. Mr. Johnson sees the collision. He agrees to testify in court to what he saw. Johnson appears and presents his testimony. Two other witnesses, Mrs. Brown and Mr. Thomas, also appear; each gives testimony which differs in detail from Johnson's. But all three agree firmly that a collision did occur and that one car went through a stop sign. All three testify that one driver is at fault; the other is innocent.

Consider first that the Christian witness also speaks

from firsthand evidence. Jesus preached to throngs of people along the Sea of Galilee, instructed his disciples parabolically and openly, mended broken lives, inspired hope in those who were mired down in cynicism, and so revealed the nature and power of God. The people who witnessed his work and heard his words—or conversed with those who did—produced the New Testament documents. But the Resurrection Christ is not locked into the first century; he is not imprisoned in a Book; he is not limited by Christian formulations of his person. The Resurrection Christ is alive, abroad, and active in this world! We, too, in our time and place, can meet the living Word (Christ) if we study the inspired human record (scriptures). We, too, can meet Christ in biblical preaching and teaching, in human conversations informed and shaped by the Word, and in the human needs that crowd in on us day after day in a society that denies justice to a third of its constituents. Any contemporary witness who speaks from these firsthand experiences of Christ can declare—as Paul did—that Christ is appealing by him. That is the essence and the dynamic of Christian witness. In some places, respectable church members, stirred by Key 73, mounted membership drives; that was inevitable. But it is not Christian witness. In wide areas of the church, the primary mission fields are the church's membership rolls; many who belong to the institution are not converted to Christ. Main-line Protestants must face the reality that conversion and growing commitment to Christ are primary needs among them; perfunctory church members are not empowered to evangelize.

Second, the use of the term "witness" reminds us that each observer of an event sees it differently. The

Christian witness does not expect *his* experience of Christ or *his* maturing life-style to be the norm for evaluating other Christian witnesses. To demand conformity is contrary to God's creative work and Christ's redemptive work. It is also self-righteous. Each Christian witness examines his own testimony against the testimony of the church through the ages, but no spokeman for Christ is bound mechanically to that corporate experience. Truth is not static. The canon of the scriptures is not closed. Dogma is not frozen. The historic Creeds and the confessional statements are historic guides to the scriptures; they are not equal with scripture.

Each Christian witness, his conscience captive to the living Word (Christ), speaks plainly from the church's experience *and* from his own experience of Christ. He evaluates the theological premises of other Christians; but he does not condemn persons whose experience and style of witness differ from his. He is open to and co-operative with all people of good will who, although marching to another drum beat, seek to improve the human situation. Intellectual arrogance, moralism, rigidity, self-righteousness, hostility, and imperialism have no place in authentic Christian witness.

Third, the term "witness" points to the freedom of the one "witnessed to." The Christian witness, seeking to persuade others to accept Christ's promises and do his commandments, accepts the fact that all human beings are free to accept or reject Christ. He discovers quickly that many who reject the gospel also reject its bearer. He learns, too, that millions of people, while respecting Jesus as a good man and a moral teacher, find meaning for their lives in another religion (Judaism, Mohammedanism,

Hinduism, Buddhism), another life philosophy (humanism), or another life-style. Not only during the Crusades and the "religious wars" of the early seventeenth century but also in twentieth-century America, members of the "Christian" church have been chauvinistic and imperialistic. It would be tragic if a new crop of "Christian" evangelists, harvested through Key 73, were to disrupt the maturing dialogue and rising cooperation between Catholic-Protestant-Orthodox Christians and the adherents of the Jewish faith. Authentic Christian witnesses, enabled by the Spirit, testify without arrogance; they argue without hostility; they differ without bitterness; they cooperate without compromise of conviction,

Finally, the word "witness" reminds us that a Christian is not God's *partner;* he is a *servant* of God's Word. His effectiveness depends in large measure on his learning to distinguish between the Treasure and the earthen vessel which holds it. When Anders Nygren resigned his professorship to become Bishop of Lund, he advised the pastors of his diocese, "We are heralds, that and nothing else." [5] That is solid counsel for Christian witnesses.

But no human being is able to herald God's Word persuasively unless he is called and empowered by Christ himself. The kingdom of God does not rely on self-appointed ambassadors. The King's man, under direct appointment, inquires daily of his Lord how he can be a responsible citizen in the kingdom and an effective spokesman for it. The Christian witness is alert to the pressures on him to accommodate the gospel to his culture. He

[5] Nygren, *The Gospel of God* (Philadelphia: Westminster Press, 1951), p. 21.

nurtures his new life from the Word and checks his insights and judgments against that Word. He realizes that unless the God he proclaims is allowed to authenticate himself in the person of the witness his testimony will limp. The Christian evangelist is haunted daily by Richard Baxter's warning, "Beware lest you be void of the saving grace that you offer to others."

Contemporary culture's preoccupation with communication—as though it were a matter only of form rather than of content and personhood as well—reveals how severely contemporary man is alienated from God, himself, and others. The Christian witness testifies from and to the common Faith; he also testifies from and to his own experience of Christ. His testimony is both report and event. His power to communicate is based not on his cleverness but on his growth in Christian and secular knowledge and on his Christian personhood. It is the whole man who communicates the gospel persuasively. In this sense only, "the medium is the message."

No Christian witness comes easily to this confidence in the content of the Faith. He must be converted to and grow in an understanding of God, self, and others. He too has traveled those roads, but he is no longer lost. *Christ has found him.* That is what he shares joyously; that is why he testifies urgently.

Christian witnessing is not reserved for an intellectual or moral elite who choose to serve God as a favor or a duty. It is God who chooses, calls, persuades, and equips his spokesmen. Consequently, evangelistic work can be done effectively by any person committed to Christ who, possessing emotional resilience and intellectual curiosity, accepts God's authority, claims his promises, honors his demands, and engages in person-to-person encounters. The style of witnessing varies from one Christian to another, but wherever church people are faithful to the Word, responsive to persons, and alert to cultural currents people in the world know from their deeds and conversation that the kingdom of God is at hand. Some persons come forward asking, "What shall I do to become a citizen of the kingdom?" Others are indifferent. Some reject the gospel outright. Each response is an evidence of *biblical* witnessing. Only as persons are truly confronted with the gospel in proclamation and demonstration will some repent, believe, learn, witness, serve.[6]

The Christian witness discovers that the forthright presentation of Christ's demands and promises creates tension, stirs controversy, incites conflict, and, on occasion, results in the rejection not only of the gospel but also of himself. This is as true in a pluralistic society as it is in a homogeneous pagan culture. It is the genius of biblical witness to expose human piety, human pretension, religion-in-general, and civil religion as enemies of biblical Christianity, usurpers of its power. When this exposure is accomplished, some persons are infuriated, others are entertained; some are indifferent, others are set to hard thinking. The *Christian* witness is not responsible for the results. It is required only that he be faithful to the Word. He is a servant of that Word, an ambassador who carries out God's orders.

This Christian witness is identified by these evident characteristics.

1. *The Christian Witness Is Honest.* Some Christians

---

[6] See Eric Routley, *Conversion* (Philadelphia: Fortress Press, 1960); it is a book written expressly for laymen.

suggest that one ought to speak only what he knows of Christ firsthand. We too have argued that one communicates the Word of God with power when he accepts Christ as his Savior and follows him as his Lord. But total commitment to Christ—full knowledge of God's will and loyalty to it—is beyond anyone. Paul himself saw through "a glass darkly." To limit one's witness *only* to his firsthand experience of Christ would warp the objective character of the gospel (what has been "delivered by the saints") and delimit its power.

The intended thrust in the plea that one should witness only to what he knows of Christ is on this order. The witness gives himself to the Word in a disciplined way. He tends to the wellsprings of his faith, searching the scriptures for God's Word to him, praying steadily for himself and others, seeking all the while to do Christ's commandments. Witnessing to God's revealed truth, serving as a steward of the gospel, he makes a witness that is objective and subjective, historical and existential.

Deliberately, we speak about the Christian witness' *honesty* rather than his *sincerity*. It is ridiculous to suppose that Christian claims are valid (or even deserving of respect) merely because they are held with sincerity. Sir James Baillie has written, "Conviction or sincerity is not a test of truth nor a guarantee of validity; it should accompany the truth but it may very well accompany error; it may be a measure of the value of ideas to the individual, but is not a measure of their validity in themselves." [7]

2. *The Christian Witness Is Humble.* Contemporary churchmen must recover the biblical concept of humility

[7] Quoted in Roy Pearson, *The Ministry of Preaching* (New York: Harper, 1959).

if they expect seriously to support God's purposes in this world. The humble man, stirred by the gospel, yearns to get free of his innate disposition to depend on himself and other selves; he hungers for Truth in his inward being, and he acts boldly on that Spirit-forged desire. The humble man prays as well as plans. He ventures recklessly for the sake of God's kingdom, trusting his Lord to use his faltering witness effectively. He searches the Bible as a means of grace; he does not venerate it as an object of faith. The humble man dares to believe that Christ is inhabiting his person and that the Holy Spirit is shaping him along the heroic lines of Christ's own Person. Confidence in God, not man, *is* Christian humility.

But Christian humility is elusive. Paradoxically, no one is in greater danger of succumbing to pride in its subtle forms than the Christian witness. Consequently, the Christian needs the redeeming power of Christ in all seasons, knows it, claims it, urges others to follow suit. "The final human pretension," Reinhold Niebuhr has reminded us, "is made most successfully under the aegis of a religion which has overcome human pretension in principle." [8]

Christian humility distinguishes between the Treasure and the earthen vessel. It does not equate the Light with the lamp.

3. *The Christian Witness Is an Unfinished Person.* He recognizes that he shares the same human condition as those to whom he ministers. Like any other mortal, he has dark nights of the soul. He is no stranger to pride,

[8] Quoted in James S. Stewart, *Heralds of God* (New York: Harper, 1952), p. 107.

impatience, arrogance, anger, bitterness, hatred, envy, lust, greed. Like any other mortal, he needs God's acceptance, forgiveness, support, and love. He declines to use his act of witnessing as a screen between God and his person or between himself and other selves as persons. He is not a holy man; he is a human servant of the Holy God.

The mature Christian witness, however, does not parade the dark hours of his soul. He proclaims Christ's Victory, not his own doubts and defeats. The disposition of some contemporary Christians to air their personal conflicts as ends in themselves obscures God's Word. One's personal witness and his closet prayer room are interdependent, not interchangeable.

The content of Christian witness is the Word—the demands and promises of Christ. The Word—heard, accepted, acted on—is the means whereby Christ makes new witnesses. The urgency to proclaim God's Word to the ends of the earth is inherent in the message itself. It is the Treasure, not the earthen vessel which contains it, that provides the *content, motivation,* and *power* for a saving witness.

4. *The Christian Witness Is Hopeful.* He brings God's judgment to bear on persons and society, but that judgment is not essentially denunciatory. The Word—good news as well as commandment—sounds the strong note of hope on every occasion. Christian witnessing makes responsive persons strong, because it testifies to the God who raised Jesus from the dead; to the Resurrection Christ who, present now on the beachheads of his kingdom, will come again to establish his kingdom forever;

and to the Holy Spirit who gathers willing persons into the new community of faith *and* hope.

Christianity promises victory to those who live in the community of Faith; the disheartened Christian crying out, "O wretched man that I am"; the despairing thief pleading, "Remember me, Lord"; the penitent prodigal asking, "Make me" instead of "Give me"; the faithful remnant in a totalitarian state asking poignantly, "How long, O Lord?" Because God has acted and continues to act in every human situation, sin has lost its power, death is swallowed in victory, all tears are wiped away. No human tragedy is beyond Christ's power to transmute it into glory. So Paul, seemingly overwhelmed by adversity, sings out: "The sufferings of this present time are slight compared with the weight of glory laid up for me." Hope is the dominant note in *Christian* witness.

5. *The Christian Witness Is a "Now" Person.* He does not live in the past or in the future; he lives *now*. The truly "now generation" is any truly *Christian* generation. The Christian, more than others, is equipped to live today fully, because God frees him of the weight of yesterday and assures him of tomorrow's victory. The Christian can do good *today* to those who injured him yesterday, because he accepts and appreciates that God has forgiven him. The Christian can endure the defeats he sustains in today's thrust for social justice, because, more than others, he accepts the empty cross as God's cosmic put-down of all injustice. The Christian, more than others, understands the rising demands of the dispossessed in America and in the Third World for "justice now." Cultural Christianity is an opiate of the people. Biblical Christianity is a revolutionary force. Whoever becomes a

new creature in Christ is motivated to join others in sharing Christ person-to-person and in bringing his insights to bear on contemporary life to fashion the just society now for the sake of the kingdom of God.

Christian witnessing is the greatest, truest, best work in the world. It is also the hardest. It cannot be done apart from God's Spirit. Subsequent chapters will underscore that reality more fully.

II
Some Common Roadblocks
to Effective Evangelism

Persons outside the church respond to Christian witness in different ways. Jesus' parable of the soils underscores that reality; our experience in the church confirms it. Many people outside the church—*and* inside—are biblically illiterate and theologicaly naïve. Others are uninterested, indifferent, hostile. Some are provincial, prejudiced, unrealistic. Others are cosmopolitan, tolerant, cynical. Yet many are searching for meaning and purpose in their lives. The late Paul Goodman was convinced that people outside the church were asking, in the 1960s, more significant theological questions than people inside the church.

Whether Goodman's judgment is accurate or not, the current situation is that the church is *not* a primary institution of society in 1974 for the majority of Americans, churched or unchurched. Unlike the family, one's vocation, the public school, and government, the church cannot command one's allegiance if he does not want it so. Any person can live a lifetime without a nod toward the church —and tens of millions do precisely that. Millions of church members have only a casual interest in Christ. Serious churchmen get depressed over the obvious irrelevance of their congregation in a pluralistic, diverse community. Increasing numbers of church members are internalizing and privatizing "their" faith.[1]

Culturally, evangelism is demanding work. Psychologically, it is frustrating and satisfying work, because human freedom makes the outcome of each encounter problematical. One aspect of man's freedom comes into sharp focus when we assemble some of the human roadblocks to effective evangelism.

I

"I Don't Need to Belong to the Church to Be Christian." That response has cropped up in every generation since Constantine. It is especially widespread in this generation. The judgment is cultural; it is not biblical.

Anyone can choose the church without Christ. Some church members manage that quite readily. But it is not possible to give one's self *fully* to Christ without accepting a responsible place with other Christ-followers in *his* band of followers who are concerned for all people everywhere. Human beings are designed to live in relationships with other persons. The New Testament is absolute on this: no person can have Christ in isolation from *other persons.*

During the 1960s it became common, especially among the burgeoning ranks of college-trained people, to declare that one had rejected the institutional church yet had held on to Jesus. But that cannot be; Christ and his church go together. Since the first Christian generation, Christ's community (which began with twelve disciples

[1] See A. Leonard Griffith, *Barriers to Christian Belief* (New York: Harper, 1962).

including Judas) has been fashioning institutional structures and singling out human leaders to equip rank-and-
file members to exercise Christ's ministry effectively. Whoever accepts Christ fully accepts his church—"warts and
all"—without necessarily approving all aspects of the
institution.

From its first beginnings, Christ's church fashioned
evangelical forms to care for persons in the community,
preserve apostolic truth, carry the gospel into the world,
and serve persons in the world. The church's historic
creeds and its doctrine of the Incarnation were fashioned
in part to refute the docetic view of Christ which makes
him less than human and robs him of historical relevance.
Christianity has been able to bridge the centuries to persons in our day by providing a Spirit-inhabited institution
through which the Word could become flesh in each
generation. The historical Jesus—a man of his times—did
not foresee the Copernican Revolution, the Industrial
Revolution, the Marxist Revolutions, nuclear weapons,
jumbo jets, or moon landings. Christ's church, however,
has lived not only to see these and more, but also to be
led by his Spirit to shape historical forms through which
Christ can confront persons in time, forms within which
the church can be Christ's body and through which it can
accomplish God's mission.

The sixteenth-century Reformation was, in part, a
criticism of the institutionalized Christianity which had
developed during the Middle Ages. But the chief reformers
did not reject the institution. They reformed it; God's
spirit renewed it. Century after century, Christianity has
brought its institutional structures, liturgical forms, and
doctrinal formulations under God's searching judgment to

discern whether they be means or ends. God's judgment is clear that the institution is not an end, but a necessary means. Institutional forms are essential means for the exercise of Christ's ministry by and to persons who are embodied spirits. One can have the church without Christ, but one cannot accept Christ fully without accepting his church.[2] Christian evangelists must get this truth across to millions of unchurched Americans.

II

"The Church Should Not Meddle in Politics." Any Christian evangelist will agree to that with alacrity. The church should not *meddle* in politics. Instead, the church, if it is to be *Christian* in the biblical sense will be *involved* directly and indirectly, actively and pervasively in political decisions which affect *persons in society:* war and peace, welfare reform, abortion laws, marriage and divorce laws, crime and punishment, penal reform, tax reform, economic imperialism, world trade, negotiations on limiting nuclear armaments, etc. The Christian church must deal with political issues knowledgeably, critically, responsibly. Everyone who finds new life in Christ is constrained not only to share that new life person-to-person but also to bring his maturing Christian insights to bear on the structures of society in order to create a just society for the sake of the kingdom of God. The Christian does not confuse the "just" society he works for with the kingdom of God. Neither does he, with an aura of self-righteous-

---

[2] See Dietrich Bonhoeffer, *The Cost of Discipleship* (New York: Macmillan Paperbacks ed., 1963), chapters 29 and 30, "The Body of Christ" and "The Visible Community."

ness, hold himself aloof from joining other people who are working for it, but are not numbered in the *Christian* community.

The Christian citizen has obligations to both church and state. But his ultimate allegiance belongs to neither institution; it belongs to God. That is Jesus' firm judgment: "Render unto Caesar . . . and render unto God. . . ." Every Christian is obliged to honor God's claim on his conscience which, acted on, may or may not affect materially the course of the state (Bonhoeffer failed) or the direction of the ecclesiastical church (Luther succeed partially). But win, lose, or draw, the Christian is obliged to honor his conscience captive to the Word of God. Biblical Christianity is not *a*-political. Contrary to popular thinking, the American Constitution actually seeks to guard the right of religion to make relevant judgments on the body-politic.

Many members in the twentieth-century American church are less knowledgeable and less interested in their political and biblical traditions than their eighteenth- and nineteenth-century forebears. Actively and passively, the Christian's attitude toward politics, economics, and social issues reflects his personal commitment to Christ, concern for persons, intellectual understanding of the gospel, and cultural realism. Many churchmen who argue that the church should "preach Christ" and stay out of politics get politically involved over issues which concern *them*. Many main-line Protestants as well as Evangelicals resisted the Supreme Court's decision on Bible-reading in the public schools. The Amish go to court when their religious views on the education of their young are threatened by the state. Some peace churches bordered on militancy in their opposition to the Vietnam War. And Protestants and Catholics alike discovered in the 1960s that conscientious objection is a political issue as well as a religious, moral, and philosophical concern. Since American Christians are citizens in a representative government, their involvement in politics is inevitable— especially if their ox is being gored.

Because people are human, the constitutional separation of church and state is positively needful. It guarantees legally that the state cannot dictate what the church's teaching and witness shall be. It also guarantees legally that a sect or denomination or an allied segment of Christendom cannot dictate that the state shall legislate in favor of that particular sect or denomination or segment of Christendom. The political lobbying of the Catholic Church to block the dissemination of birth control information among the citizens of Massachusetts and Connecticut during the 1950s and 1960s was a violation of the principle of "separation of church and state." On the other hand, Protestants lobbied for Bible-reading in the public schools in violation of the First Amendment. Jefferson—Father of the Statute of Religious Freedom in Virginia, 1786 (the precedent for part of the First Amendment to the Federal Constitution)—would be distressed by the political naïveté and casuistry of many contemporary churchmen and by the rigid secular prejudice of some unchurched citizens who argue jointly that the church should be disallowed from speaking on political issues. That would disenfranchise half the citizenry! It would also compromise the church, for when it declines to speak to human concerns, it denies the Incarnation and the Lordship of Christ.

Interaction between the institutions of church and state is inevitable because (a) Christ redeems persons who live in political societies; (b) Christians are citizens of the state; (c) politics is a means of establishing order and promoting justice among peoples; (d) the Constitution guarantees freedom of religion, speech, press, and assembly. The legal separation of the institutions of church and state safeguards American society against secular-minded citizens and church-oriented citizens who, in varying circumstances, seek to enact or endorse coercive measures through either institution, church or state. The current flight from political responsibility in some quarters of the church (its membership comprised of citizens) is contrary to the letter and the spirit of the Constitution. Neither politics nor piety can be compartmentalized. Our forebears recognized and accepted that reality. As responsible citizens and honest churchmen we must accept it too.

The church, viewed biblically, exists to preach and teach Christ, guard apostolic truth, care for persons in community, and refashion society so that anyone who wants to can become truly human. This fourth task, the humanization of persons, cannot be accomplished in an urban-technological society without enlightened, responsible government action. The church bears a measure of responsibility for seeing that this action occurs.

Conservative churchmen are also getting more involved in politics. Floyd Robertson, assistant to the general director of the National Association of Evangelicals, declared recently: "Our involvement in government affairs pertains only to those things which directly affect the function of the church and its activities—mission, chaplains, taxes, education, and freedom of speech as it pertains to radio and jail ministries." [3] Lobbying by the National Association of Evangelicals focuses on issues which concern the church institutionally. But the *political* orientation is there. Mr. Robertson has also stated: "We will . . . encourage the introduction of legislation which we feel to be of particular interest to the church as a whole or to *individuals as citizens*." [4] The Evangelicals' fortnightly journal, *Christianity Today,* hints invitingly at open doors for dialogue and cooperation with main-line Protestants on social issues.[5] George McGovern attracted some outspoken Evangelicals during his presidential campaign, and there were "peace kids" at Expo '72. Sherwood Wirt, editor of *Decision,* published by the Billy Graham Evangelistic Association, argues persuasively in a solid study of the Evangelicals' social conscience that these earnest Bible-grounded churchmen are waking from their "Rip Van Winkle sleep" and are poised for social involvement.[6] Each community of faith must reassess its own traditions, gain fresh insight into its brothers' traditions, and get on with God's work here and now. It is in doing that work, more than in dialoguing between and

[3] James L. Adams, *The Growing Church Lobby in Washington* (Grand Rapids: Eerdmans, 1970), p. 139.

[4] *Ibid.,* p. 139. The italics are mine.

[5] A rapprochement between liberal and conservative Protestants—as well as Protestant cooperation with Catholics—is crucial to the Christian church in America if it is to "come of age" as a concerned, ecumenical community in an urban-technological society. Jews and humanists must be respected allies, too, in the Christian church's concern for peace and justice.

[6] Sherwood Eliot Wirt, *The Social Conscience of the Evangelical* (New York: Harper, 1968). See especially chapters 3 and 10-14.

among traditions, that true community comes into being.

The Christian evangelist will also take pains to point out to the prospective member who is confused on the issue of church and state that the Christian church has room for all persons who, accepting the biblical principle of social-political involvement, apply it honestly and responsibly as their consciences dictate. It is in this arena of colliding judgments and convictions that the Word of the Lord can come into focus for us in our era. Subtle and strident demands that the church withdraw from contemporary social and political arenas is a demonic call for a twentieth-century pietism that has no precedent in the Old and New Testaments.

Some responsible churchmen argue that the church must restrict itself to motivating persons from the gospel to reorder society; they question church statements, pronouncements, directives, direct actions, and lobbying.[7] But this view has proved to be irrelevant in the technological nation-states of the twentieth century. Suppose the American church had taken up the cause of labor in 1886. Suppose the German church had spoken corporately and specifically to the Nazi state in 1934 and shared its judgments with the world community of Christians. Suppose the Vatican had spoken for the Jews in Hitler's state in 1937. Suppose the American church had spoken

[7] See Jacques Ellul, *The Politics of God and the Politics of Man* (Grand Rapids: Eerdmans, 1972); Paul Ramsey, *Who Speaks for the Church* (Nashville: Abingdon Press, 1967); Helmut Thielicke, *Theological Ethics: Vol II, Politics* (Philadelphia: Fortress Press, 1969); Will D. Campbell and James Y. Hollaway, *Up to Our Steeples in Politics* (paperback ed.; Paramus, N.J.: Paulist/Newman Press, 1970) for cautions against aggressive church involvement in politics.

concertedly against the Vietnam War before 1964. Suppose the American church had given concerted support to welfare reform which the Congress buried in 1970. In each case it is conceivable that a significant historical impact would have been made. At least, the image of a church that cares about persons would have been projected in the world; the church's prophetic utility would have been exercised. The best time for the church to speak is not at the gate of Auschwitz but before the camp is erected.[8]

Basically, the demands of God underlie the historical necessity for the church to provide directives on specific issues. In every historical situation prophetic opposition to any government's inhumane policies is inherent in the church's commitment to the gospel. Jeremiah was rejected by his community because he spoke for God to concrete social and political issues. Amos and Micah were jarringly specific about God's demands for justice to the poor in eighth-century Israel. John the Baptist suffered capital punishment, because he identified specifically the immoral behavior of Herod. Jesus, accepting the woman taken in adultery as a person, forgave her; he also directed her to sin no more. He called Herod "that fox," the Pharisees "whited sepulchers," and forcibly ejected the moneychangers from his Father's house. Directives *and* direct action have a strong place in Christian faith and life. Both law and gospel comprise God's Word.

When the church is true to the gospel, it speaks concretely to specific social issues. Biblical tradition supports that sweeping assertion. Since social questions be-

[8] See Wallace E. Fisher, *Politics, Poker, and Piety* (Nashville: Abingdon Press, 1972), especially chapters 4 and 5.

come political issues (especially in a democratic society) and since churchmen are citizens, at least a segment of the church will express its views publicly; it will bring them to the attention of government officials; and, like other segments of American society, lobby for them. That is a constitutional exercise. It is also authentic biblical witness.[9]

III

"The Church Asks for Money." Of course it does. People are not "souls with ears." Man is not a disembodied spirit. Americans are not nomads who live in caves or under movable tents. A majority of American citizens do not reside permanently in the place of their birth; American society is mobile, especially since World War II. But Americans, while moving from place to place, do reside in well-appointed trailer homes, modest and expensive apartments and town houses for five, fifteen, or thirty years. The churches in our society are permanently located; congregations meet in buildings, buy furnishings, claim utilities, and employ full-time personnel. Consequantly, the church needs money. It is that elemental.

Most laymen in the 1970s desire competent professional leadership in their churches. Our way of life depends on specialized services: professionals in the law, medicine, teaching, ministry, plumbing, building, research, etc. In order that these professionals can utilize their talents and training fully, those who want their services provide for their material support through salaries, wages,

[9] *Ibid.,* chapter 5.

fees, perquisites. Culturally, the provision for the income for doctors, lawyers, teachers, secretaries, contractors, plumbers, bricklayers, and realtors rests on society's need for specialized services. The same principle operates in all of them. The church, like other social institutions, needs money. And if the local congregation's ministry is to be carried into the community and beyond its boundaries, money will be needed for necessary buildings and equipment, and more professionals. The church needs and therefore asks for money. How could it be otherwise?

The criticism that the church asks for money is, for many people, a defense that thinly masks their selfishness, provincialism, insensitivity. Because the church is a voluntary association, people can, and many do, claim and demand the services of the church at substandard costs compared with what they pay for competent services in other fields. This double standard hardens the church member's heart and wounds the full-time church worker's psyche. A forthright discussion of giving to the church is an essential strand in effective evangelism. This aspect of Christian life should be discussed realistically in each class for new members.

But this is only the first stage of the conversation about the church and money; there is a larger field for confrontation.

It is the nature of man to adopt a material way of looking at persons, experiences, and objects. Jesus, keenly aware of this, spoke five times more often about money than about prayer. Natural man judges too much on what he sees, hears, feels, tastes, and smells. Americans, poor and well-to-do alike, are consciously and unconsciously materialistic. Overwhelmed by an overabundance of material goods, plagued by built-in obsolescence, and goaded by high-pressure advertising (directed skillfully to exploit envy and greed), the majority of Americans live by material values. The Christian church, beginning with its evangelistic thrust into the world and ending with its lifestyle of servanthood, must provide a constant challenge and a sane alternative to contemporary America's material way of looking at life. Ecological reform, for example, will not occur in any significant sense until a majority of Americans alter radically their internal value system. Christian stewardship and Christian evangelism are inseparable! [10] Unless one over-spiritualizes the church, which is unbiblical, one cannot talk about the church without discussing money.

On the other hand, there are grounds on which the honest critic of the church can take the offensive against the evangelist in a discussion about the church and money.

First, some prospectives will ask to examine the budget of the evangelist's congregation. If that budget is unrealistic, niggardly, they may charge the congregation's leadership and rank-and-file members with irresponsibility. In the church in the Third World material sacrifice is a mark of Christian commitment. That is also true in some corners of America—urban ghettos, Appalachia, Indian reservations, etc. But among three-quarters of America's citizens, half of whom are church members, benevolence and current gifts are substandard. Increasingly, prospective

---

[10] See Fisher, *From Tradition to Mission* (Apex Books; Nashville: Abingdon Press, 1974, [1965]), chapter 5, for an extended description of an urban congregation's arduous climb from a $38,000 annual budget to a $385,000 annual budget.

members will challenge that lack. The evangelist must be prepared to handle this relevant criticism honestly.

Second, more and more prospectives will ask bluntly, "Why do you seek support for a faltering congregation? What right do you have for asking others to give money to keep your congregation in existence? There are too many struggling churches in this community now. Why don't you merge with several other congregations?" The honest evangelist must be ready to answer this inquiry which will become increasingly common during the 1970s.

IV

"There Are Too Many Hypocrites in the Church Now." Before we respond to this spurious criticism on scriptural grounds we remind the reader that no Christian ever employs that threadbare quip: "Come in. There's always room for one more." That response is ungracious; it is also unbiblical.

The word "hypocrite" (Greek), means "one who affirms publicly what he does not believe privately, one who pretends to possess virtues which are not his." Literally, a hypocrite is an actor, a pretender, a dissembler. Jesus used the word bluntly in face-to-face encounters with religious pretenders. But he did not call Peter a hypocrite; he did not imply that Judas was a hypocrite. He saw both men as sinners, human beings who had missed the mark, undisciplined men following the dictates of their egos rather than his promptings.

So, the Christian evangelist gets down to cases. He talks about church membership in terms of sin and grace, illusions and authenticity of personhood, frustration and satisfaction, emptiness and fulfillment, present imperfection and ultimate perfection. Williston Walker, church historian of yesteryear, said that the church is not a museum for perfected persons but a hospital for sick humans. Henry Ward Beecher, an eminent Congregational preacher after the Civil War, said that "the church is not a gallery for the exhibition of eminent Christians, but a school for the education of the imperfect ones." Dr. Beecher, given to amorous affairs outside his marriage, demonstrated the truth in his description! Simon Peter, who promised so much and delivered so little until he surrendered his ego to Christ, belongs in the gallery of Christian Faith. In that gallery the only occupants are forgiven sinners.

Scripture underscores the human frailties of the Christ-believers. It reports unhesitatingly that Judas, part of the nucleus of the new community, defected and that every apostle faltered badly now and again. The New Testament does not hide the dark stains and gray patches on the fabric of life in the early Christian community: Peter denied his Lord; Ananias and Sapphira cheated; Demas quit; John Mark ran home for a season; the Corinthians were stingy; the Galatians were taken in by false teachers. And Paul—often impatient, occasionally angry—called a time or two for excluding church members because they behaved immorally.

The difference that sets off a church member from others is his relationship with Christ. Bonhoeffer observed that church members "wander on earth and live in heaven, and although they are weak, they protect the world; they taste of peace in the midst of turmoil; they are poor, and yet they have all they want. They stand in suffering and remain in joy, they appear dead to all outward sense and lead a life of faith within." [11]

To call the church "holy," therefore, is to have one's eye fixed more firmly on Christ and his gospel than on man and his performance. The church is holy (acceptable to God) when the Word is preached, taught, listened to, heeded, embodied in the believer's person, and acted on in the world. The church is not a human invention; it is God's idea. Christ is the foundation of this new community; it is his Body on earth. "The church . . . is a fundamental part of the divine purpose, willed by God and established by him just as much as the incarnation itself . . . The church, therefore, is a vital part of the gospel itself." [12]

Biblical teaching sets it down firmly that the kingdom of God has already come. On the other hand, scripture also teaches that the kingdom is yet to come in its fullness. The church, therefore, reminds people that the kingdom, already present, is a triumphant task; it also points to the kingdom yet to come, a future gift in the all-embracing victory of Christ. The church militant—sometimes marching with banners flying, sometimes retreating ingloriously—lives on and points steadily to that victory that was won in that cosmic "pay-off" battle at Calvary. And when the Resurrection Christ, the life of the church, appears in all his glory, his followers "too will appear in glory with him as princes of the earth. They will reign and triumph with him, and adorn heaven

---

[11] Bonhoeffer, *The Cost of Discipleship,* p. 304.
[12] Langdon Gilkey, *How the Church Can Minister to the World Without Losing Itself* (New York: Harper, 1964), pp. 60-61.

as shining lights. Their joy will be shared with all." [13]

Sinners constitute the church. But they are "hypocrites" only if, confronted daily by the righteous demands of Christ, they resist deliberately his better way.

V

"I Can't Accept the Christian God Because He Allows Injustice, Destruction, and Death in the World." There are at least two levels at which the Christian evangelist will address this pervasive concern which plagues so many earnest people—and disturbs mature Christians on occasion.

A. Many people are honest in declaring that they cannot get a perspective on "a good God and an evil world." Essentially, the problem is theological. The Christian evangelist may choose to address it along these broad lines.

Because human beings are finite, ignorant, and ego-centered, life—with or without God—is riddled with error, pain, and death. The rain pelts the just and the unjust. It is simple realism to recognize that human sin frustrates God's purposes in history. But it is absurd to reject God because of man's inhumanity to man. It is unreasonable to flail at God because our perishing planet "faults" at times. In the long run, it is as fool-hardy to ignore the dangers of maintaining San Francisco over a scientifically known *earth fault* as it is for a person to jump from the Golden Gate Bridge in blind defiance of natural realities.

[13] C. F. Richter. Quoted by Bonhoeffer, *The Cost of Discipleship,* p. 304.

Nonetheless, each evangelist must address this plaintive charge against God issued by many people now outside the church. Recognizing that it is a shallow "intellectual" dodge for some and an honest question for many, the evangelist will wrestle with the charge against God's goodness in the light of Calvary's Cross and in accordance with the evangelist's personal theology on personal hardship, human suffering, and "natural disasters." There is no textbook answer.[14]

B. The second level of addressment is historical—existential. Everyone has wounds, and countless persons have been mauled unmercifully by life. The Christian evangelist hears these anguished, angry, bitter cries:

> "My son was killed in an air raid over Hanoi three days before Christmas, 1972. And you talk to me about a *good* God?"

> "My friend, an executive in an oil company in Dallas, was forced to resign his position because he described the harsh atmosphere of Dallas at the time of John Kennedy's assassination."

> "My lovely wife died of cancer when she was twenty-four."

> "My husband, a kind man, suffered a disabling stroke at forty-one and hasn't worked since."

> "A drunken driver ran down my seven-year-old daughter; she is permanently invalided."

> "My college classmate, now an able Christian minister,

[14] However, some laymen will find helpful Leslie D. Weatherhead, *Salute to a Sufferer* (Nashville: Abingdon Press, 1962).

was forced to resign his pastorate in Birmingham in 1963, because he was active in the cause of civil rights."

"I lost my advancement in the corporation because of politics in the 'executive suite.' "

"I worked in the church for years, but my husband lost his job and can't get another at fifty-two. Now, we've lost our home, our savings—everything. It doesn't pay to go to church."

These hard-pressed people with existential questions —and the first group with their intellectual questions— can be joined in responsible, meaningful, compassionate conversation on these counts.

(1) The gospel enables us to accept the ego-shattering truth that human suffering is often *punitive*. It is the consequence of man's abuse, disuse, or misuse of his freedom. The historian is blunt: "The mills of God grind slowly but they grind exceeding fine." Jesus, too, does not mince words: "What a man sows, he also reaps." Of course, guilt is not only personal; it is also corporate. To live is to be caught up inextricably in the web of human association. To live in an affluent society is to sin against starving people in India. The corporate abuse of human freedom may be more damaging than the personal abuse of freedom. Suffering—personal and corporate—is often punitive.

(2) Biblical Christianity teaches that suffering can be *remedial*. This is one strand in the book of Job. Jesus also makes it plain that the "new life" is not based on a mechanical system of rewards and punishments, but on one's relationship with him—in good times and bad.

If one is placed in this world for the purpose of

maturing into the kind of person who loves freely and witnesses gladly without concern for recognition or reward, the remedial aspect of suffering makes sense. If man is set in the human situation to learn how to live comfortably with God forever, remedial suffering is essential in that dynamic process. George Eliot, no stranger to suffering, wrote, "It would be a poor result of all our anguish and wrestling if we won nothing but our old selves at the end of it." Job in adversity was closer to God than Job in prosperity: "Though he slay me yet will I trust him." Suffering *can* be remedial. In our affluent society where so many value comfort above character and honor convenience above conscience, remedial suffering makes sense to those who believe in the God who calls them to authentic personhood.

(3) The gospel of God also teaches that voluntary suffering, accepted for Christ's sake, is *redemptive*. Jesus could have bypassed Calvary. Paul, after his Damascus Road experience, could have returned to the Sanhedrin. Schweitzer could have had his pleasant academic life. Wesley was not compelled to share the hardships of the eighteenth-century English proletariat. Bonhoeffer could have remained at Union Seminary in New York City in 1939.

To take Christ seriously means costly discipleship. Suffering, for Christ's sake, is always redemptive.

(4) Biblical Christianity also suggests that some suffering is unexplainable, incomprehensible to any finite being. Paul sets it down flatly that the most mature Christian sees life in a warped mirror; his picture of events is distorted. This kind of suffering does not result from God's displeasure; it is simply a strand in an imperfect

world. It's just the way life is. Philosophic stoicism can make this suffering bearable (Marcus Aurelius). Confidence in God can transmute this inexplicable suffering into exciting witness (Job).

Deep suffering breeds loneliness; it causes isolation. Unshared, it can destroy one's person. Every sufferer needs a Friend who understands him and his predicament. To be truly understood is a strengthening experience. When the pianist Grieg composed the musical score for Ibsen's poem "Peer Gynt," Ibsen, hearing the score for the first time, gripped Grieg's hand and whispered, "Understood! Understood!" Christ, the High Priest touched by all our infirmities, understands our suffering, shares our suffering, enables us to transmute our suffering into deathless character and persuasive witness.

The Christian evangelist will not persuade everyone in this deeply wounded segment of society to follow Christ, but he can go right on caring for these people—and praying for them.

VI

"I Was Forced to Attend Church as a Child. I've Had It." The Christian evangelist will probe at this response kindly but firmly to determine whether it is a petulant evidence of the prospective's emotional and intellectual immaturity or an honest expression of psychic hurt. If it is the former, the evangelist will initiate and attempt to carry on a fruitful examination of every human being's need for personal growth and emotional maturity.

On the other hand, if the evangelist suspects strongly that the prospective member may have been psychically damaged in his youth, he inquires gently whether he may ask his pastor to call. Most prospectives will agree to have a minister visit. It is the "professional's" task to determine during his conversation whether he can help the person or whether the prospective needs a psychiatrist to liberate him from that and *other* childhood prisons. This, too, is a strand in person-oriented evangelism.

VII

"I Don't Need the Church: I Get Along Quite Well on My Own." The evangelist will be honest: millions of people live without Christ, know little or nothing of his gospel, and are *not* cracking up. In fact, some are more humane, concerned, and involved with persons than millions of our fellow church members. The Christian evangelist knows that and admits it candidly. But he carried on the conversation, if allowed the opportunity, orienting to these biblical focuses.

A. Sin. Man is saddled with a towering ego; he is a sinner. The unity of man is shattered. His freedom is despoiled. He is alienated from his fellows. This schism occurred when man, created for fellowship with God, banished his Creator from the citadel of his inner life and set up his own ego on a makeshift throne. This rebel government is unable to maintain harmony in man. Each facet of his personality wars against the other facets. Paul agonizes over this awful schism: "I do not do the good I want, but the evil I do not want is what I do" (Rom. 7:19 RSV). Everyman's inner civil war throws him into competition and conflict with his fellows, and they with him.

The biblical story of man's fall—rescued from liberalism's cavalier attitude toward sin and freed from biblicism's inability to differentiate myth from history—tells how man, violating his freedom by rejecting God's sovereignty and grace, fell into bondage to his own conflicting instincts, hungers, and aspirations. Man cannot bridge "the ugly ditch" that he digs between himself and God. The *London Times Literary Supplement* observed several years ago that "the doctrine of original sin is the only empirically verifiable doctrine of the Christian Faith." [15] Carlton J. H. Hayes, late professor of European history at Columbia University, argued that every historian must acknowledge the doctrine of original sin. Whether historians acknowledge the doctrine, ignore it, or deny it, they record its consequences!

The biblical record, of course, provides massive evidence that there is a tragic flaw in man. Natural man, the scriptures report matter-of-factly, is in rebellion against God, his fellows, and himself. Consequently, he denies the rights of others and often claims them for himself. Consequently, he acts against his own best interests as well as those of others. Every human being has a mercurial reason, a conscience like quicksand, a will dedicated to self and to provincial interests. The Christian doctrine of original sin reflects accurately man's actual experience of himself and other selves. C. G. Jung warned four decades ago that modern man's civilized state was veneer; the evils of primitive man, he insisted, were crouching in the recesses of his heart. The Communist purges in Russia and China, the Nazi ovens, and the American napalm bombs in Vietnam burned that truth into the human

[15] The *London Times* was, in fact, quoting Reinhold Niebuhr.

consciousness. The human disposition to evil can be demonstrated empirically, but modern man has not been able to agree on the locus of his trouble or the nature of it.

B. Liberation. Christ liberates man; he saves him from sin. Jesus, accepting sin as a reality, pointed to its mysterious power. He revealed its depth, tenacity, hatefulness, and death-dealing power. He tracked it home to the innermost part of man—the human will. Face to face with Christ, man's human pretensions are exposed in bold relief. When Christ confronts man-the-rebel and demands that his motivation conform to God's holiness, the issue is cleanly defined; no human being is able to meet that demand.

There is a chasmic difference between John Gardner's plea for human excellence and Jesus' plea for righteousness, between human sacrifice and God's sacrifice on Calvary. Perfectionism, the other face of self-righteousness, roots in self-centeredness. So every human creature is hoisted on his own petard. His desire to be God *is* sin. Only God can rescue man from himself. Only God can forgive man's transgression, heal his alienation, persuade him to end his rebellion. Only God, the injured party, can close the books on man's offenses against him and his family. This he has done in Christ.

Modern man needs pardon, insight, direction, and meaning because he is mortal, finite, perverse. He needs a new set of affections, humane goals, selfless motivation. He needs acceptance, understanding, love. The poet-anthropologist Loren Eiseley has observed: "No creature in the world demands more love than man; no creature is less adapted to survive without it."

That is the good news: "God so loved the world that

he gave his only Son . . " It was man's desperate *need* for love calling out to God's immeasurable capacity to love that moved the Almighty to do what he did in Jesus Christ. Because man cannot be truly human until he loves, because he cannot love until he is loved, and because he cannot will to do good until he is enabled to will it, Christ did for man what he cannot do for himself.

Long ago, Plato remarked that "we must take the best and most irrefragable of human doctrines and embark on that as if it were a raft on which to risk the voyage of life—unless it were possible to find a stronger vessel, some Divine Word on which we might take our journey more surely and with confidence." The Christian evangelist has *that* Divine Word, "a raft on which he risks the voyage of life" and helps others to climb aboard.

VIII

"It Doesn't Make Any Difference Which Church You Join as Long as You Are Active." This popular notion that every church is equally good for everyone is psychologically unrealistic, socially naïve, and theologically untenable.

Churches, like people, are different. In many instances they are radically different. This is reality. These differences stem not only from their different views on and interpretations of the scriptures but also from their different attempts to relate the biblical message directly to the needs of persons in their moment of history. The lifestyle of Rose Kennedy, for example, differs from the lifestyle of Billy Graham. This is true *in part* because Catholic Christianity formed Mrs. Kennedy while Baptist Christianity shaped Dr. Graham. On the other hand, the Berrigans were also shaped *in part* by Catholic Christianity, and Harvey Cox was nurtured in the Baptist faith. Human beings—differing in intelligence, sensitivity, emotional resilience, vision, cultural heritage—are not only attracted to and choose to live in different churches, but they also respond differently to the teachings in the same Christian tradition. Presently, both Catholics and mainline Protestants are finding it necessary to appraise and come to terms with "pentecostalism" in their midst.

A church that focuses on the "personal" gospel influences persons in a fashion different from a church that focuses on the "social" gospel. And a church that accepts Christ and culture in tension (a "personal-social" gospel) fashions a third temper of mind which is radically different from the other two! A church that looks on liturgy as a cultic rite shapes people differently from a church that views liturgical forms as flexible human means to worship the holy God. A church that examines one's faith in terms of doctrinal subscription fosters a mindset radically different from that fostered in a church which examines faith as existential engagements with doubt and despair throughout life.

Different people with different expectations choose different churches. They also mature differently in the same *tradition,* because they differ in their response to different stimuli and in their capacity to grow.

Dillenberger and Welch, in their classic study, *Protestant Christianity,* define this reality with clarity.

> The fact of diversity in belief and practice is a striking part of the Protestant heritage. Men think different

thoughts even when they seek to witness to the same gospel. This may be due to human creativity and human finitude; even more it may be due to prideful men who think too highly of their own outlook upon life. Protestantism accepts this ambiguity as a part of its heritage. It accepts its diversity as a sign of health and of sickness. Even in the ecumenical movement, where men are keenly conscious of the broken and divided nature of the churches as the body of Christ, the fact of necessary difference is accepted.[16]

First, persons schooled in the liberal arts and/or critical-minded by nature cannot participate—at least whole-mindedly—in any church committed *rigidly* and closed-mindedly to a literalistic view of the scriptures.[17] We are not implying that the sincerity of the nonpartici-pants is larger than that of active fundamentalist church-men. We are simply recognizing that many people are "turned off" by biblicistic, doctrinaire churches. We rec-ognize just as readily that committed biblical literalists are deeply suspicious of confessional churches that orient to a dynamic (as opposed to a static) doctrine of the Word of God, and they are positively inimical to "liberal" churches that "preach causes rather than Christ." These differences are real. They must be admitted openly, exa-mined objectively, and discussed candidly without ar-rogance, bitterness, or self-righteousness. Any "church" that denies the Spirit of Christ ceases to be *his* church.

[16] John Dillenberger and Claude Welch, *Protestant Chris-tianity* (New York: Scribner's, 1954), p. 1.

[17] We are not speaking here of Evangelical churches in general but of "closed," fundamentalist churches outside the scope of Wirt's study, *The Social Conscience of the Evangelical.* See above, footnote 6.

Second, some people are more comfortable in urban congregations because temperamentally and culturally they prefer to rub shoulders with people who are socially and economically different from them as well as with those who are like them. We are not suggesting that the quality of Christian life in the center-city and inner-city churches is superior *per se* to the quality of Christian life in the suburban churches. We are recognizing the fact of personal preference, sound or unsound. This is how one member in a center-city church expressed her personal preference:

> Only in a church like ours can I be part of a truly heterogeneous community—heterogeneous in age, racial, social, economic, and educational levels. Our children, privileged in so many ways, rarely acquire this advantage because of our surburban location, except in _____, where we experience real community.

It is also necessary to recognize that many people prefer the suburban church. Their choice too is conditioned culturally and psychologically. We may get a measure of insight into the complex character of cultural-psychological preferences in general if we examine one of the thorny problems which small, isolated American towns face these days in trying to get a physician to reside in their comfunity. With few exceptions, American doctors attend medical school and intern in large metropolitan communities. There, many of them learn to appreciate the theater, ballet, symphony, etc. The sincere desire of some young doctors to serve people in America's small isolated communities collides with their desire to locate where their own cultural needs are met more adequately. Cultural-psychological needs define the choice of a church for many people.

There are also practical reasons why people prefer the suburban church. Families with several young children, for example, find it more convenient to join a church near home. Most teen-agers prefer churches where their classmates attend. Elderly persons find it more convenient to unite with nearby congregations. Many men who drive to the center city five or six days a week prefer a church close at hand. And many people are hesitant to attend an urban church in a changing neighborhood.

When a prospective member admits (as most do if the evangelist listens) that he is attracted to a particular church because it is convenient, or is filled with his kind of people, or nurtures his established outlook on life, the effective Christian evangelist will encourage him to examine his reason(s) for his leaning. One need not be boorish or overbearing to encourage prospectives to examine their impressions, notions, and feelings about suburban or urban churches before the tribunal of biblical evidence. One should join a church for objective as well as subjective reasons.

Third, some churches are more intellectually oriented in their preaching-teaching-dialogue ministries than others. Riverside Church in New York City, under Harry Emerson Fosdick in the 1930s and early 1940s, was decidedly more intellectual than most Protestant churches in America in those decades. That is not a denigration of the ministries in other churches; it is recognition of reality. During the 1940s and 1950s, Reinhold Niebuhr attracted overflow crowds to the Harvard Chapel, President James B. Conant among them. In the 1950s and 1960s, Billy

Graham filled Yankee Stadium in New York City and Harringay in London with 100,000 night after night. The difference in intellectual content and cultural context between the sermons of the two preachers was one reason for the difference in human response. I am not implying that either preacher was "better" than the other. I am pointing out that not only congregations, Christian traditions, and Christian teachers differ in their intellectual orientation and content but also that Christian laymen differ in their capacity to appreciate and absorb Christian preaching and teaching that stretches the mind as well as touches the heart and challenges the will.

Obviously, a congregation's over-commitment to intellectualism or emotionalism or moralism fractures biblical Christianity. Churches which glory in being anti-intellectual also demean the biblical image of ministry. Nonetheless, these different emphases do exist in differing degrees, often to an extreme degree, in many churches. And each congregation attracts some people while it repels others. Imbalance in ministry is a constant threat to the whole Word of the Lord getting to people.

Fourth, some people seek out a congregation that is involved actively in the secular community; they want a pulpit that addresses social and political issues concretely in the light of God's Word. The turbulent 1960s produced fruit. Many laymen want to be responsibly involved in society. On the other hand, many people continue to be attracted to the custodial congregations which maintain "chaplains in residence" to minister primarily to the "spiritual" needs of their members. The prophetically involved *and* the custodial congregations exist side by side in our American communities. Neither type will disappear

in the 1970s. It is crucial that they accept each other
honestly and communicate openly. Meantime, both will
seek to propagate their interpretation of Christianity.
Every lay evangelist will challenge uncritical prospectives
who think that all churches are the same. In reality, the
difference (theology, liturgy, social involvement, life-
style) can not only transform a member's life but also
influence society itself.

Christ's church does indeed exist wherever the Word
of God is shared through preaching, teaching, and the
sacraments; where two or three persons, or two or three
thousand people respond affirmatively to God's deed in
Christ; and where church members serve persons in the
world. But the theological foundations, accent on the
gospel, style, and tempo of one's own congregation are
different in degree from those same aspects in every other
congregation, and different in kind from others.

IX

"I've Outgrown Christianity." Friedrich Schleiermacher's cultured despisers, an elitist band in his day, are
legion in 1974. Their well-filled ranks are swelled annually by tens of thousands of college graduates. The
clergy and a select corps of lay evangelists in each congregation must cultivate a concern for and fashion a
strategy to approach persons who feel that they do not
fit into the cultural molds which the institutional church
appears to espouse, or who consider themselves part of the
counter-culture.

It is not possible in these brief paragraphs to examine carefully this burgeoning field for evangelism.[18] But we can provide some hints on identifying the cultured despisers and on addressing them. (a) Thousands of educated Americans, exposed to a college course on world religions, consider all religions equally sound for their adherents (educated Americans are "tolerant") and equally false for them. But that is only one strand in understanding and addressing a person who at nineteen rejected Christianity on "intellectual" grounds. The evangelist must probe deeper. (b) During their adolescence, thousands of cultured despisers were members of congregations which throttled human minds, exploited human emotions, and manipulated human wills. This disillusioned segment of American society, locked by dated emotions rooted in caricatures of Christianity, is especially difficult to evangelize. They are dealt with best, if at all, through long-term one-to-one dialogical relationships. (c) There are thousands of people in America for whom the God of their childhood simply became too small as their experience in life broadened and deepened. These cultured despisers are best approached by evangelists who are able to present existentially the majestic God of creation, the historic God of the Israelites, and the gracious God and Father of Jesus. (d) Millions of people in American society are cultured despisers of Christianity not because they had a religion course or two at the

[18] See Wallace E. Fisher, *The Affable Enemy* (Nashville: Abingdon Press, 1970). This little book—encompassing a collection of letters between a business executive (in the church) and one of his university professors (a Christian)—examines casual commitment to Christ, the cost of discipleship in contemporary society, compartmentalized religion, and anti-intellectualism in the church. The book is beamed to the cultured despiser.

University, or because the church of their youth
caricatured God, or because their God became too small,
but because their egos are larger than the actual dimen-
sions of their intellect. The Christian evangelist is as concerned to work with and persuade these persons as he is
to work with and persuade other persons to Christ. Experience suggests that the evangelist working with these
persons needs—in addition to commitment, understanding
of the gospel, and cultural realism—an extra measure
of patience and *a sense of humor!*

X

"I Don't Want a Religion that Cramps My Style."
The largest segment of American society to be evangelized
in the 1970s is populated by those who are in love with
this present world *as it is.* One remembers here the
concise biography Paul penned of his fellow-evangelist,
Demas: "Demas hath forsaken me, having loved this
present world, and departed for Thessalonica." Demas
gave up his evangelistic work with Paul, because he pre-
ferred the everyday life in bustling Thessalonica—its daily
action, its sights and smells and sounds, its worldly talk,
its idle gossip. That disposition to sensuality and mediocrity
is deep-set in human nature. The Israelites, who yearned
to escape the heel of the Egyptians, followed Moses
eagerly at first; but when they faced starvation they
wanted to return to bondage in Egypt where they ate
reasonably well. Jesus pointed out that many people offer
thin soil for the growth of the gospel, that they are
particularly susceptible to the cares and pleasures of this
world which choke off the gospel's growth.

Every church member knows people like this in the

community where he lives. "Churchy" evangelists are tempted to live and let live, declining to challenge these persons to serious Christian conversation; or worse, they harangue and belittle them. The evangelist's best approach to these one-dimensional people, at least initially, is indirect; he lets his style and quality of life have its impact. He waits for his neighbor to inquire into the source of his new life.

Every Christian ought to have the name of one of these persons on his conscience, ought to befriend him, ought to pray for him daily. Serious evangelists will be steadied for long-term engagements of this sort if they remember that Augustine lived for years with one foot in the camp of the cultured despisers and the other in the world of sensuality. Monica, his mother—with her indefatigable prayers—and Ambrose, Bishop of Milan—with his well-furnished Christian mind—finally won Augustine to the Christian community. In Christian history, that one-time cultured despiser and dashing rogue stands second only to the Apostle Paul!

Then there are the Blacks, the poor whites, the uneducated, the prisoners, the uncouth, the cast-offs, and the alienated whom main-line Protestants rarely evangelize and only recently have shown even casual concern for. Perhaps in this decade, only sectarian Christians, urban Protestant and Catholic churches, and special ministries will seek out these teeming millions for Christ; but if that be true, the church, under God's judgment, will wane. Its integrity, relevance, and effectiveness are already suspect in all quarters of society; and millions ignore it as a museum piece from another cultural era.

That is the theme of the next chapter.

III
The Integrity of the
Evangelizing Congregation

We are agreed that the Christian evangelist does not sell himself to or press his congregation on the prospective member. He presents Christ and his gospel, person-to-person, in cultural context. That is his essential task. The evangelist is the earthen vessel which carries the Treasure to persons in the world; some accept the gift, others decline it. But the Christian witness is not a loner; he is part of a fellowship, a congregation of believers which is the body of Christ inside society—and of a worldwide fellowship constituted of thousands of local congregations.

God committed his gospel to the community of Christ-believers and Christ-bearers. In person-to-person evangelism, one's witness to Christ is communal as well as personal. The evangelist, proclaiming the gospel, wants the "prospective" member to accept Christ, worship him, learn of him, and serve him in and through his church. The evangelist's concrete goal is to persuade prospectives to unite with a particular congregation.

As a matter of integrity, the Christian evangelist is concerned that those who unite with the congregation he represents shall be cared for effectively from the resources of God's Word. He is not a P. T. Barnum convinced that "a sucker is born every minute." He is not a nineteenth-century drummer who, committed to the cynical philosophy, "Let the buyer beware," hoodwinks his prospective. He is not a Madison Avenue huckster who, relying on motivation research, manipulates his candidate into the church. The Christian evangelist is, in one sense, a "spiritual Ralph Nader" determined that his new member will receive *effective care* in the congregation he joins.

Across the centuries, but especialy since the nineteenth century, a mountain of books has appeared under titles like these: *Pastoral Care, Pastoral Concern, The Care of Persons, The Cure of Souls, Shepherding the Congregation,* etc. These books were written by clergymen for clergymen. They are uneven in value, but lay evangelists would profit from reading in one or two of the better works.[1] Realism suggests, however, that most evangelists will not get to reading a book like this, discussing it, or acting on it. So, we shall be plain in discussing the effective care of persons.

Recall the phrase that appears in some obituaries: "She was under a physician's care." Recall the achievement or failure of the fourteen-year-old boy whom the court had placed in the care of foster parents in your congregation. Recall the time you read that a British jet which crashed on take-off from Heathrow had been under the care of the airline's maintenance crew that same day. Recall your neighbor who was fined because he did not care properly for his German shepherd. Recall the divorces you know of firsthand which occurred because one or both mates did not care for the other.

[1] Daniel Day Williams, *The Care of Persons* (New York: Harper, 1958) is an especially competent work—readable, solid, concise.

To care for someone or something requires more than a "feeling" for that person. To care for another human being is to provide for him, attend to his needs, perform personal services for the good of his person. This requires compassion, commitment, competence. Compassion without competence and commitment is ineffectual. Commitment without competence and compassion is cold. Competence without compassion and commitment is sterile. Employing these tests, the witness can determine whether his own congregation cares for persons or only claims to care for persons. This is a crucial strand in evangelistic work; the integrity of the evangelist and his congregation are at stake.

"Integrity" is a tarnished word in the American vocabulary. That was not always so. There was a glowing season in American society when a person's word was as good as his bond; neighbor trusted neighbor and most American citizens boasted about their social-political institutions. That was yesterday! In 1974, there is a raging sea of distrust between the races and the classes, between conservatives and liberals, between mates, between parents and children. There is bitter distrust between the American people and their once respected social institutions— the public school, the government, the church.[2] A credibility gap between the American people and their political institutions has developed over the last two decades. Violations of public trust have escalated steadily: Harry Vaughn's five-percenters, Sherman Adams' wheeling-dealing, Bobby Baker's blatant dishonesty, the Viet-

[2] To appreciate the changing image of "the American," see Fisher, *Politics, Poker, and Piety,* chapter 3, "The American," pp. 61-88.

nam War, Attorney General Kleindienst's efforts to gloss over the ITT scandal and Watergate. These and other revelations about the government have soured millions of Americans on their political institutions. A substantial segment of American citizens does not trust the promises or programs of any political leader. In the crucial election of 1972, almost half the eligible voters did not turn a hand to put either candidate in the Presidential office.

Meanwhile, Catholics and Protestants discovered that some of their ecclesiastical leaders (ordained and lay) had obscured some truths deliberately, had manipulated church members to get monies for programs and buildings, and had placed institutional needs above human needs in far too many historical situations. Consequently, the church, like other social institutions, has become for millions of people part of the social problem rather than part of the social answer. The church has created its own credibility gap. Its integrity is badly tarnished in every corner of society, especially among the young, the poor, the minorities, and the social actionists. The care of persons in some Protestant and Catholic congregations is not effective; worse still, it is hurtful in many cases.

I

Certainly, one evidence that a congregation cares effectively for persons is the competent way it enables laymen to get at the Word of God in the words of men, to discern God's activity in history, to meet Christ in scripture. But that is not being accomplished effectively in most congregations. Almost a hundred years after solid biblical scholarship had equipped clergy in main-line

Protestant churches to discern the Word of God in the words of men, there are thousands of churches ministered to by men and women who, though trained in biblical criticism, have not shared its constructive results with rank-and-file church members. Consequently, biblical illiteracy or biblical authoritarianism characterizes most Christian congregations. The laymen's need to learn to get at the Word of God in the words of men is not being met responsibly in the twentieth-century church. Effective care in this crucial area simply is not provided in most congregations.

Theologically, Protestants agree on the seat of authority: *sola scriptura.* But Protestants as well as Catholics are "hung up" on the nature and interpretation of that authority. The authority of scripture, long obscured for Catholics, is badly blurred for Protestants on three levels: the dead hand of particular denominational-sectarian *traditions* ("frozen" Christianity); the relationship between the scriptures and the Word of God (how to discern the Word of God in the words of men); and the interpretation of the scriptures' witness to God's mighty deeds (historical or existential—or both; social or personal—or both).

The self-acknowledged conservative churches and sects are getting into deep water over the nature of scripture's authority, too. This growing wing of Protestantism has begun to look critically at traditions which may be culturally rather than biblically rooted. The younger clergy in these churches are examining the scriptures in the light of biblical scholarship and human need in a dehumanized society. A segment of "conservative" laity is also engaging in bold acts of social service and social protest. A minority of clergy and laity are getting involved politically. Controversy seethes beneath the surface in the once placid gatherings of the conservatives. Baptists, Brethren, Mennonites, Missouri Lutherans—and scores more—are now experiencing the travail which Methodists, Episcopalians, United Presbyterians, the United Church of Christ, and a branch of Lutherans (LCA) experienced in their theological schools several decades ago. But the clergy in these latter churches have neglected to encourage fully the general church membership to face the implications and claim the fruits of sound biblical scholarship. Too often these enlightened clergy have neglected the tedious but necessary task of enlightening the laity.[3] A misread Bible concerns enlightened Christians as deeply as an unread Bible; the first fault is more destructive than the second.[4]

But how shall evidence be taken before the tribunal of biblical evidence? Who rules on the evidence? In what sense, substance or form, is scripture inspired? Is the Bible the Word of God or does it contain the Word of God? What is the relation between the Word of God and the words of men? If God's self-revelation is progressive (through myths, legends, historical events, the prophets, and Christ)—and the record demonstrates that it is—how can all scripture be of equal authority? Since Christ is the full expression of God's self-revelation in history, is he not the only sure guide for interpreting all scripture? If

[3] See Fisher, *From Tradition to Mission,* chapters 3 and 4, for an account of sharing the insights of biblical scholarship with a congregation.

[4] Church history and modern psychiatry provide firm evidence for this claim.

a congregation is to provide effective care for its members, the clergy and laity must wrestle with these questions at the parish level. A responsible congregation teaches its members how to get at the Word of God in the words of man; it also teaches them how to interpret scripture.

We are not implying that biblical scholarship provides a magical formula for new life in the church. But, as a tool, it enables the church to preach and teach, to learn and do the Word effectively. It helps to introduce persons to the fundamentals of the Faith, especially the fundamental: "God was in Christ reconciling the world to himself."

II

Clergy, educated in the doctrines of the church, have neither effectively encouraged the laity to examine doctrines critically for their relevance today, nor helped to recast them in meaningful forms for technological man in the nuclear age. The former Anglican Bishop John Robinson, popularizing his version of Bultmann and distorting Bonhoeffer, made that abundantly clear a decade ago.[5] Church doctrines—man-made formulations of aspects of Christian truth—reflect, and are therefore bound to, the culture of the era in which they are fashioned. Unless they are explained cleanly or recast relevantly, theological naïveté and shallow moralism will continue to prevail in the American parishes. The integrity of the church has been badly compromised because professionals

[5] *Honest to God* (Philadelphia: Westminster Press, 1963). See also his *Human Face of God* (Philadelphia: Westminster Press, 1973).

have failed to interpret and recast church doctrine for intelligent consumption at the congregational level.

III

A decade after Michael Harrington's *Other America* was published, the church, in spite of some significant involvements in the 1960s, is in the rear guard of the lagging fight against poverty. Except for the sects and occasional main-line Protestant churches in urban centers, most congregations do not seek out poor people as members. And the main-line Protestant churches—their "paying" ranks recruited from middle-income and upper-income families—are not aggressive in attacking the social problem of poverty in an urban-technological society.

Fifteen years after the publication of John Kenneth Galbraith's *Affluent Society* (which called for a radical reappraisal of national priorities), the church is only now, and only in a few places, challenging solidly the value judgments of the American people and how they establish priorities for the expenditure of government and church funds. Here too the middle-class congregations themselves (Protestant and Catholic) are a substantial part of the problem. The members orient to a materialistic philosophy in their own living situations. They question welfare for the poor and endorse corporate welfare (the saving of Lockheed) which benefits the well-to-do. If Jesus' ethic is taken seriously, these congregations constitute a mission field ripe for the harvest. The church should remember humbly that the clamor to reorder priorities on military spending came initially from the poor and the youth, most of whom were *not active in any church*.

Integrity requires the congregational leadership, ordained and lay, to re-examine its economic, social, and political foundations in the glaring light of God's Word.

IV

Almost three hundred years after John Locke enunciated his social contract theory and two hundred years after his writings influenced the framing of the American Declaration of Independence and the American Constitution, the church's constituency remains committed to the view that the law of the land exists *primarily* for the protection of private property. A generation after Roosevelt's New Deal endeavored to place persons above property, and almost a decade (1965) after the government acted to protect and extend human rights (legally), the church—except for a minority—still clings to John Locke rather than to Amos and Jeremiah!

The church, promising to care for persons, is often more interested in protecting property than in caring for persons. I am not attacking the concept of private property or the need to safeguard it by law. I hold no brief for the communist or socialist ideologies. I subscribe to a responsibly regulated system of free enterprise that is not dominated—as it is today in America—by a handful of corporate giants and conglomerates. The point I am seeking to make is that the church lags far behind those humanists, agnostics, atheists, and minority Christians who insist vigorously that the American government, under the Bill of Rights, is at least as responsible for protecting human rights as for protecting property rights. Many "Lockean" churchmen were more concerned about the destruction of property in Watts, Newark, Detroit, Washington, and at Kent State and Jackson State than they were about the loss of human life or the moral failure which preceded those riots.

V

Three decades after the nuclear holocausts in Hiroshima and Nagasaki, the church, except for some "peace churches," has scarcely stirred itself to think seriously about the personal and social implications of technological warfare. The concept of a "just war" is uncritically accepted among the Protestant and Catholic laity who also endorse uncritically the American military-technological-industrial complex. To the churched as well as the unchurched the American sovereign state must be supported when it is at war. Hundreds of thousands of young people and Blacks challenged this view in the 1960s, but it was a relatively small segment of the church that spoke out against the Vietnam War before 1968. Few main-line Protestants or Catholics are wrestling presently with the issue of nuclear war.[6]

The integrity of the church is suspect in all these social-economic-political areas.

VI

One of the most glaring areas where the church's integrity is suspect in the care of persons is in its definition of church membership. Few congregations exhibit serious

[6] See Fisher, *Politics, Poker, and Piety*, chapter 4, "Dissent in America."

concern that all their members should worship, practice stewardship, evangelize, get socially involved, and grow in the likeness of Jesus' humanity, and in that process demonstrate Christ's transforming love *in the church and in the world*. They accept without real concern that 60 to 70 percent of the members commune; 30 percent worship; 8 percent give responsibly; 1 percent evangelize; .02 percent get involved in social ministry; .01 percent speak out at personal risk to themselves. Any other social institution would go out of business on that performance record!

The membership policy in force in any congregation reflects that congregation's commitment to Christ, biblical knowledge, theological understanding, and concern for persons. National church bodies, Protestant and Catholic, have one set of requirements for the clergy and another for the laity. In most churches the standard for the laity is dictated pragmatically: it is a base for levying an annual apportionment. In few congregations does the policy reflect a serious concern for the nurture of the members in the Faith. Since it is the local congregation which sets or declines to set membership requirements, and since churches differ denominationally, and since congregations in the same "tradition" differ, no one policy is fostered in these pages. Our aim is to get each congregation to give this matter serious attention; congregational integrity is at stake. Here are four kinds of policies currently in force in Christian congregations.

First, most main-line Protestant churches rely on a dual membership roll: active and inactive members. Some refer to the inactive list as "a conscience list." Here and there a congregation works steadily to reclaim the laggards, but most of them only go through the motions. There is solid evidence that the "active-inactive policy" exists in most congregations (a) to keep the apportionment down and (b) to avoid confronting inactives face-to-face with the demands of Christ.

Second, a handful of main-line Protestant congregations and several sects have membership policies that are ruggedly demanding. New members are admitted to the fellowship only after they engage in an extensive study of Christianity, a probationary period, and their personal promise to worship weekly, study the Bible daily, evangelize, tithe, serve persons, and pray regularly. One of the more widely known congregations with a policy along these lines is The Church of the Saviour in Washington, D.C. Critics of their policy argue that its formulators, in their zeal to encourage responsible churchmanship, have confused the church militant with the Kingdom of God. These critics judge that the policy, strictly applied, turns the church into a sect.

Third, some congregations covenant annually to worship faithfully, to give generously, to serve responsibly. Those who "sign up" each year are counted as "members" for the coming year. Peace Lutheran Church, Arlington, Virginia, is a pioneer in this. Critics of their policy argue that it is too permissive.

Fourth, Trinity Church, Lancaster, Pennsylvania, has fashioned a policy that the clergy, vestry, and parishioners judge to be a strong *aid* in their multi-faceted effort to care effectively for persons.[7] Critics of the policy argue that it is legalistic. Clergy and vestry deny the criticism

[7] See Appendix I, pp. 119-125.

because of its evangelical content and the pastoral way it is administered. Many clergy and some laymen in and beyond Lancaster have asked for copies of the policy and have applied it fully or in part in their situation.[8] Trinity's policy emerged from the congregation's new life after seventeen years of the present ministry. It was conceived, formulated, revised, and written by the twenty-one lay persons on the vestry of Trinity Church. We think it (a) distinguishes properly between the kingdom of God and the church militant, (b) respects human freedom, (c) takes seriously the integrity of Christ's church, and (d) expresses the pastoral and lay leadership's concern that all members be encouraged to claim the promises of Christ and accept his demands reponsibly.

The policy has been in force since January, 1970. The "book membership" (adult) has declined 10 percent. The average attendance at worship (over 1,100) and in the church school (600-plus) has inched forward. The annual giving has climbed from $295,000 to $380,000 in spite of a $22,000 loss (monies provided by former members) as a result of the application of the policy. The *congregation's* social involvement in and beyond the community has deepened. The prophetic style of the *congregation* has sharpened. Twenty-one persons who surrendered their membership in Trinity have united with other congregations in Lancaster and other communities. A dozen or so have returned to active membership in Trinity. The others, to our knowledge, attend nowhere. Mean-

---

[8] We have distributed, on request, over 1,100 copies of the policy to clergy and laymen throughout the nation and in eastern Canada.

time, a hundred or so casual members in Trinity have taken the responsibility of membership more seriously. The membership policy, shared with all prospective members, has discouraged few and encouraged many.

VII

Consider next the pulpit in providing effective care of persons. Prospective members and resident members of a congregation, hard-pressed in life-situations, expect comfort from the preaching in their church. That is a proper expectation. But the word "comfort" means "to make strong," and that has a price tag.

If a responsible cadre of citizens in an urban community sets out to make their downtown area attractive, inviting, and livable, they experience hardship. First, it is necessary to demolish inadequate buildings. Next, acres of land must be cleared and streets must be widened. Third, a comprehensive design must be approved. Fourth, the rebuilding of the area must be pushed to completion. Each of these steps is marked by frustration and travail, tension and conflict. Satisfaction and fulfillment are by-products of *doing* the job effectively.

An effective preaching-teaching ministry is like that. Preaching strengthens people only if it communicates the Word, and the Word of the Lord cuts before it heals. God's Word demolishes ego-habitations; that is devastating. It levels and widens one's inner being; that is disruptive. Its flexible design for living (the mind of Christ) must be adopted; that is demanding and often ambiguous. Building the new life in Christ is painful each step of the way; the project goes awry frequently. Repentance and faith, frustration and satisfaction, failure and accomplishment, sorrow and joy are strands in that building process. Through it all, the only solid ground for hope is the Builder, Christ. He who initiated the good work will bring it to completion.

Preaching that only tears down and levels is not Christian preaching. Preaching that focuses *exclusively* on peace of mind, personal security, or social action is not Christian preaching. Preaching that ignores the human need for a Savior is not Christian preaching. Preaching that ignores elemental human needs in this world is not Christian preaching.

No congregation cares effectively for persons inside or outside its fellowship through its formal preaching until that preaching shatters the old ego, levels and widens the inner life, underscores God's design for living responsibly in his world and caring for persons, and builds the new life in Christ. If the preaching in any congregation orients to *single goals* like peace of mind, social action, personal security, Bible reading as a project, or winning new members it cannot provide God's full care for persons.

The laity, and especially laymen engaged in evangelistic work, need to converse with their clergy and fellow-members concerning the nature of biblical preaching. The ablest, committed clergy need the support, constructive criticism, insights, encouragement, challenge, and prayers of their fellow-Christians if the clergy *and* the laity are to preach the Word of God. The laity as well as the pastor(s) determine whether a particular congregation hears and then preaches God's Word in the world. Biblical preaching is a cornerstone in the effective care of persons. The responsibility for it rests not only with the clergy and official board but also with the congregation.

Clergy and laity alike must examine periodically the balance or imbalance of the formal preaching in their congregation; biblically rooted, it appeals to the mind, heart, and will. Preaching that fosters anti-intellectualism is not biblical. Preaching that is coldly intellectual, every ounce of emotion squeezed out of it, is not biblical. Preaching that is largely emotional is not biblical. Preaching that centers only on concrete evils in society is not biblical. When the Word of God is at the center of the pulpit the preacher is constrained to challenge, prod, and encourage the whole congregation to examine *all* human experience *and* historical situations in the light of the gospel. If one is open to the Word, he cares for persons; his witness becomes particular, specific, concrete, personal, effective.

VIII

An examination of the teaching ministry in any congregation reveals whether effective or ineffective care is being provided for the members. There are at least three facets of the congregation's teaching that must be examined: (1) curricula, (2) shepherding, (3) the commitment and competence of the teaching staff.

Since most congregations use curricula provided by their denominational boards of parish education, and since this study book is oriented interdenominationally, I shall make only guideline suggestions. First, the congregational committee on parish education should be alert to materials provided by other denominations and secular sources to supplement, correct, enrich, and balance the solid materials provided by their own denomination. Increasingly, congregations are fashioning some of their own materials for use beyond the seventh-grade level. Most congregations are alert to adapting *all* materials so that the teaching is relevant to the cultural experience of *their* students. Second, responsible shepherding of the students by ordained and lay persons is absolutely essential to a serious, effective teaching ministry. Regular attendance is crucial. Third, the commitment and competence of the teaching staff is the largest single factor in the effective care of persons through teaching. This requires thoughtful choice, education (biblical and theological content), training, teaching skills, and steady pastoral encouragement. At Trinity Church a plainly written "call" for lay teachers has been useful since 1961.[9]

IX

Integrity is also violated when persons and congregations are casually mis-mated. This is a messy issue, but congregations will face it if they care honestly for persons.

The falling-away of church members in the mainline Protestant and Catholic churches during the last decade or so roots in multiple causes—some evident, some ambiguous. One identifiable cause is the simple fact that many people are not mated properly with the congregation into which they were born or which they joined uncritically in adult life. Church membership, in one sense,

[9] See Appendix II, pp. 126-27.

is like a solid marriage; it matures, in large measure, because of compatible mating. As a considerate, quiet divorce is a sane solution to mismating in marriage (if professional counseling has failed to bring the couple together), a change in congregational membership, carefully thought out, discussed openly with the clergy and some laity in both congregations, and acted on decisively, is the only hope for saving hundreds of thousands of people to the Christian community in the 1970s.

Many people, coming into a new city or town, take membership in a particular congregation without careful, prayerful thought. Millions of members on church rolls— an accident of birth or a casual choice in adult life— live on the periphery of their congregations. Their pattern of worship is random, their giving is nominal, their witness is negative. Yet many of these people would mature as Christian persons in other congregations of the same denomination, in other denominations, or in different theological-ecclesiastical traditions.

Hundreds of thousands of church members must seek membership in another congregation (or denomination, or Christian tradition) *in the same community* if they are to mature in the Faith. That practice must become an essential strand in Christian evangelism for the 1970s. Acceptance and application of this principle will require a radical change in the thinking of many clergy and most lay leaders. It will also require grace and guts to act on it! Some Christian congregations do act on this principle; and they are stronger for it.[10] It is a strand in the effective care of persons.

[10] Trinity Church has acted on this principle for twenty years. See Fisher, *From Tradition to Mission,* pp. 101-18.

Lay evangelists and clergy should encourage prospective members to give at least as much attention to the choice of a church as they do to their choice of a new car, a wedding gown, an investment stock, or the place for a family holiday. If and when that happens, the church will take a giant step forward. The responsibility for challenging people to make realistic choices rests primarily with the professional and lay evangelists in every Christian congregation. This is a matter of simple integrity.

One clear demonstration that a congregation is truly concerned for persons (and *is* in fact ecumenical) occurs when evangelists Willard and Janet Smith, seeking to persuade Edwin and Kathleen Brown to take up membership in their church, Christ United Methodist, discover that the Brown family is likely to mature more steadily in the First Presbyterian Church and encourage them to unite there. Presently, only a handful of congregations evangelize in that fashion.

At Amsterdam (World Council of Churches, 1948), Protestant Christians declared: "We plan to stay together." At Evanston (World Council of Churches, 1954), they declared: "We plan to live and work together." In the 1970s, especially in America, local congregations and denominations are being forced situationally to work and live together openly and responsibly at the grass roots; they are being compelled situationally to cross parochial, denominational, and Reformation boundaries. Under the triple pressures of institutional survival, the responsible care of members, and wrestling with human needs in a technological society, American churches are beginning to translate yesterday's bold ecclesiastical declarations into realities. But, the pace is too slow; Christian evangelists must quicken it. This openness to and cooperation with others for the purpose of improving the human situation is yet another evidence that a congregation cares effectively for persons. It is a solid way for the church to bridge its credibility gap.

X

There are, of course, many other areas in which evangelists can and should examine whether the care of persons provided by their congregation is effective. Is the music in our congregation so "pure" (Bach, the standard of judgment) that hundreds of people are turned off in their honest desire to worship God? Is the music in our church so self-consciously contemporary that it is one-dimensional, banal, flat? Is the counseling ministry in our congregation competent in meeting some human needs and enlightened enough to refer persons to specialists when that is necessary? Is our congregation's church school a rival "congregation" or a *school,* competently staffed, in which serious students learn of Christ, dig into theology, and examine and discuss social issues in the light of the Word for sixty or seventy-five minutes each Sunday? Is the order of worship meaningful to our congregation? Is it varied enough to give persons a choice?

These and related questions, asked and worked on, demonstrate the local congregation's honest concern for persons. No congregation has the right to expect people to invest their lives in it, and no evangelist has the right to invite persons into its membership unless that congregation provides effective care of its members from the resources of the Word—*and* cares actively for persons in the world who never choose to join its fellowship, or any other Christian fellowship.

God so loved the world. . . . His Son's church cannot afford to do less without violating its integrity and caricaturing Christ.

That is the theme of the next chapter.

IV
Laymen and Clergy in the 1970s

We have examined the dynamic, content, and varied styles of evangelistic work. We have identified and addressed some of the reasons our contemporaries offer for declining membership in the church. We have described the evangelist's responsibility to be alert and open to his congregation's effective care of persons. In this chapter we shall identify twelve areas which define a changing church in a changing society. Cultural realism, we have agreed, is the third element in effective evangelism. The social changes identified here should be discussed in the broader context of the radical cultural change identified in chapter 1.

It was comparatively simple, given the scientific data on launching, to predict when manned rockets would land on the moon. It is incalculably more difficult to predict what a particular segment of human beings will do next year, next month, or tomorrow. In fact, it is impossible for anyone to predict what he will do in this or that situation in the next hour or so. Sometimes we do better than we expected; on other occasions our performance is less than we had hoped it would be. Paul, deeply conscious of this element of unpredictability in human nature, declared flatly that he would throw in the sponge except for Christ's power to steady him.

Precise social predictions are impossible because human events outrun or under-shoot the predictions of the keenest prognosticators. In a 1969 issue of *Atlantic* magazine, John Kenneth Galbraith, writing about his influential book, *The Affluent Society,* ten years after its publication (1959), stated candidly that he had had no notion in 1959 that a racial revolution would engulf America during the 1960s. Precise social prognostication is impossible. The popular notion that electronic devices will eventually eliminate all error from life is equally misleading. Electronic machines are not *people*-proof. Don Darling, a consultant on electronic security systems, declared flatly: "What it comes down to is that there are no final solutions in the security business. The practicing scientists and engineers are not even reducing crime. We're just filling up the moat with electronic alligators." [1]

The human element simply is not predictable in the absolute sense. But broad judgments can be made and, if held tentatively and handled flexibly, provide a sense of direction. Here then are some clues culled from secular and religious literature and from leadership participation in over 140 conferences of clergy and laity in a dozen different denominations throughout the United States and Canada during the last decade. This brief outline can be expanded, corrected, and discussed by the study group.

I

Church members, like unchurched persons, will be intensely concerned about realizing their humanity—and

[1] Quoted in Roger Rapoport, "Electronic Alligators," *The Saturday Review of the Sciences,* March, 1973, p. 43.

they will insist on doing it in *their own way,* although this almost neurotic insistence could produce a new "conformism." Millions of Americans will concentrate on achieving authentic personhood as individuals and fashioning meaningful social relationships. They will not be satisfied to define themselves only in terms of their vocation or profession, marriage, citizenship, or denominational allegiance. The hucksters on TV, aware of this new emphasis, are already playing up "the real me," "the one life" theme. Millions of Americans will seek their true identity in meaningful relationships with persons inside, but especially *outside,* their working experience. This widening search for personhood will generate confusion, conflict, alienation, reconciliation; hopefully it will produce candor, compassion, tolerance, acceptance.

Christians are convinced that firm direction will be discerned—and a sense of community will emerge—among those who accept God's description of true humanity in the person of Jesus and seek to have Christ's mind in them. Two decades ago John Baillie put that conviction into prayer form: "Let me love Thee, as Thou didst first love me; and in loving Thee let me love also my neighbor; and in loving Thee and my neighbor in Thee let me be saved from all false love of myself." [2] But the healthiest Christians will be restless, and the strongest Christian congregations will sound an uncertain trumpet in this decade—or longer. But it is possible, if churchmen follow hard after Christ *and* keep their wits, that the 1970s will see a theology of faith take shape even as the 1960s witnessed the lineaments of a theology of concern, a theology

[2] John Baillie, *A Diary of Private Prayer* (New York: Scribner's, 1949), p. 83.

of politics, and a theology of hope. As "future shock" envelopes the world citizenry, millions of people in the church and government and education who have been trying to turn back the clock, or to check the pace of change will discover that neither task can be accomplished. Increasingly, as churchmen seek to realize their true humanity they will discover that unless they live by faith and hope they will not be able to live at all. The alternative will be a variant of George Orwell's *1984* at worst, or Aldous Huxley's *Brave New World* at best. And B. F. Skinner is convinced—and he is convincing others—that either nightmare can be made personally palatable and socially productive.[3]

II

Church people will be less disposed to depend unhealthily on institutional Christianity. Responding and relating to emotionally secure and emotionally troubled persons, to changing social circumstances and political situations, many churchmen will treat institutional forms as means rather than ends. They will insist that this view shall prevail in their synods, dioceses, districts, conferences, presbyteries, and national church bureauracies. They will not disdain institutional Christianity, but they will simplify, streamline, and flexibilize local, regional, and national structures to accomplish a clearheaded, swift, effective ministry to persons. They will welcome creative help from any source, but they will resist *direction* from the "top" down. They will be disposed to work things out

[3] B. F. Skinner, *Beyond Freedom and Dignity* (New York: Alfred A. Knopf, 1971).

for themselves in cooperation and in conflict with their
neighbors and regional colleagues. Diversity, not conformity, will prevail in church structures and programs
in the 1970s. "The Organization Man" whom William
Whyte described so accurately in the early 1950s will
still lurk in the wings, but his influence will wane in
church circles as it waned in business circles a decade
ago, and hopefully, will wane in government circles during this decade.[4]

III

Churchmen will view "ministry" in broader terms
than they did in the 1950s (institutional) and the 1960s
(social action). The majority of ordained clergy in the
1970s will continue to be parish pastors, church admin-
istrators, and professors in theological seminaries, col-
leges, and universities. But additional special ministries
(college and military chaplaincies; ministries to subcultural
groups—young, aged, drug users, prisoners; chaplains at
recreational resorts; etc.) will win new supporters and at-
tract new practitioners. Consequently, these ministries will
take on a larger significance for the institutional church.
This will be especially true of the church's specialized
ministries to youth in the 1970s.

There are exciting possibilities in these specialized
ministries; there are also dangers. Theologically alert
churchmen will recall Luther's pertinent observation that
while all Christians are priests, not all Christians are

[4] Christian laymen ought to examine critically "The Pentagon
Papers," current revelations about the CIA, political use of the
FBI, etc.

clergymen. The current social predicament and the gospel's constraint to minister to all people, especially oppressed people, will broaden the church's presently confused concept of ministry; it will also help to bring it into focus. The American church will discover at long last that not all "ministers" of Christ need to be clergymen. The results of that discovery are promisingly unpredictable.

Another evidence of this widening concept of ministry is that the evangelical churches are getting more involved socially and politically. Their massive Congress on Evangelism in Minneapolis in 1969 declared firmly that evangelism in the 1970s must be linked to social concerns.[5]

IV

Increasingly, a substantial bloc of ordained clergy will view themselves as "professionals." A widening corps of laity approve this new professionalism and encourage it; more and more churches will demand it. To the degree that this new self-image encourages the clergy to review pastoral skills and competence critically; to accept and participate in continuing education; and to discuss the effect of their ministries openly with fellow-ministers, other professionals, and lay leaders, this change will be salutary. But a *thoroughly* professionalized clergy could damage severely the sense of vocation which, in the judgment of the writer, is indispensable to the dynamic biblical image of ministry.

[5] Recall chapter 2, part 2.

For good and ill, this new professionalism will result in church workers' more aggressive negotiations for adequate salaries, housing allowances, continuing education, and sabbaticals.

V

Main-line Protestant and Catholic churchmen, ordained and lay, will be more interested in theology during the decade of the 1970s. In the 1960s, a sizable bloc of clergy—and educators and politicians—struggled courageously to understand the "now generation" (youth, Blacks, disadvantaged whites) who deliberately split experience from knowledge (historical, theological, sociological) and placed uncritical confidence in experience. The clergy ranks themselves were enlarged year after year with this new breed. The McLuhanites are now peopling contemporary society as the scientists peopled the last several generations of Western society.[6] The central *critique* these people make is sound: knowledge without experience can be sterile—and often is. But experience without reflective knowledge loses value.

It is indeed true that experience without knowledge is frustrating; occasionally it is destructive. Paul admonished the early church to link zeal with knowledge. That is sound counsel, necessary for churchmen, educators, politicians, and parents in the 1970s who will be more sensitive and alert to Paul's dual concept: experience plus knowledge.

[6] It is challenging to reflect on the fact that Marshall McLuhan needed 100,000 *printed* words to disseminate his thesis.

VI

Churchmen will continue to adopt pragmatic approaches to ministry as readily as they apply theological principles to it. Experimentation in inner- and extra-church relationships will accelerate during the 1970s. Pressing human needs and rising socio-economic-political dilemmas will force local congregations, synods, dioceses, and councils of churches to join forces with concerned groups whose ideological and/or theological convictions are moderately or radically different from their own. Historically, alliances of this sort have proved to be mixed blessings. This will be true in the 1970s. The commitment, concern, intelligence, and realism of persons in some communities will guarantee that these cooperative ventures will be orderly and productive. In other communities, partly because the problems are larger and the ambiguities of the social situation are sharper, they will be messy and disruptive. But, for good and ill, the *tempo* of change in church relations will quicken in the 1970s among main-line Protestant and Catholic churches.

VII

Most clergy in large, well staffed, socially involved congregations and in custodial congregations will give more attention, energy, and work to the public proclamation of the Word.[7] At the same time, the ministries to subcultures will give no attention to preaching in the formal sense. But hundreds of thousands of Christian assemblies meeting on Sundays and increasingly on week-

[7] See Fisher, *From Tradition to Mission,* chapter 3.

day evenings will expect ordained ministers to preach "sermons"—to proclaim the Good News publicly. Laymen will expect to be enlightened, nurtured, and equipped from the Word through the preaching ministry as well as in teaching-counseling-social action encounters. These are their lifelines for living meaningfully, serving persons effectively, and fashioning humane sociopolitical structures.

In the main-line Protestant churches—and among the Evangelical churches and sects—evangelism will be joined more realistically with social action. This will be especially evident in the preaching of the seventies. The proclamation of the Word will be viewed increasingly as a function of ministry to be exercised by the laity as well as the clergy. It appears that this proclamatory aspect of evangelism will be more pronounced during the seventies than it was in the fifties and sixties.

VIII

The clergy will exhibit a larger flexibility as "professionals." This new flexibility will emerge from their deepening dependence on Christ (situationally constrained and theologically encouraged), widening personal-professional experience in secular society, and rising appreciation of what it means to live as concerned persons in a pluralistic society, more disciplined personal reliance on scripture and prayer, and the rising expectations of some of their parishioners. Role-playing will diminish. This larger flexibility will lead to wider cooperation between and among churches at the grass roots. It will also stake out new arenas where the church's innovative ideas and fresh convictions will collide sharply with contemporary cultural values.

Historically, the American church—as main-line Protestants, Catholics, and Evangelicals dialogue and co-operate more fully—may develop a "sectarian" style during the 1970s on the order of, yet less distinct than, the confessing church in Nazi Germany after the Barmen Declaration of 1934. In the grass roots church there may be more, although less dramatic, "local" Berrigans, Stringfellows, Groppis, Coffins, Browns, and Bonhoeffers.

IX

More clergy will be interested in serving on staff ministries in large congregations and/or in team ministries created and supported by cooperating congregations in the same denomination or across denominational lines. This will increase specialism in the parish ministry. Thousands of generalists will continue to serve parishes, but the number of specialists in the *parish* will soar. Correspondingly, through the merger of smaller congregations and the demise of other congregations (economic rather than simple common sense) as well as this changing desire among ministers themselves, there will be a reduction of "solo" ministries during the 1970s.

X

Laity and clergy at the grass roots will press with vigor for the reordering or corporate priorities in the American economy. They will badger their national churches to act and, at the grass roots, they will challenge their fellow-Christians and fellow-citizens to ask not only whether certain products are harmful but whether various products are good for people or useful as advertised. Belatedly, ecology will win thousands of champions among church members in the 1970s; unfortunately, some will take up this Christian concern as an escape from the equally pressing issues of racism, poverty, and creeping totalitarian government.

XI

Both clergy and laity will be more critical (evaluative) of psychology, socio-psychology, and sociology in relation to their own competence as ministers of the Word and as Christian evangelists. Inclined since World War II to accept these disciplines as "saviors," alert churchmen, especially clergy—while utilizing the contributions of all three disciplines and remaining open to their continuing contributions—will bring these disciplines before the tribunal of biblical evidence to determine the strengths and limitations of each for *Christian ministry*. The clergy will examine whether their emphasis is on *pastoral* or *counselor* in their counseling ministry. They will question whether sensitivity sessions, unless guided by professionally trained persons, are helpful; they will be especially skeptical of occasional sessions of this sort. They will be as concerned to understand the church biblically and to describe it theologically as to view it sociologically.

These three shifts in emphases promise a resurgence of evangelical Christianity in the 1970s. Conservative, confessional, and liberal churches will benefit from that. The church may be more true to its biblical character in America than it has been in decades.

XII

Both clergy and laity will be, by necessity as much as by choice, more concerned with the relationship between church and state (cooperation and conflict) than they have been since the days of the Young Republic. The church, like Belgium in World War I, could be "cornered into greatness."

The issue of church and state is an old chestnut in medieval and modern European history. More venerable yet in Christian history, it reaches back to Jesus' declaration: "Render unto Caesar . . .". Oscar Cullmann states categorically that "the question of Church and State . . . is so closely bound up with the Gospel itself that they emerge together." [8]

The ambiguous character of church and state tensions is being thrust at churched and unchurched Americans whether they want it or not. The significant relationship between Christ and culture, faith and political action, belief and patriotism, piety and politics is an integral strand in the fabric of American society.

The most recent cleavage between church and state in America (by no means, the first) surfaced during the 1950s. It came into sharp focus in the 1960s. Two Supreme Court decisions in the 1950s—one *directly* (prayer and Bible-reading in the public schools) and the other *indirectly* (equal integrated public education)—made church people in particular and the citizenry in general freshly aware of the age-old church-state controversy.

[8] Oscar Cullmann, *The State in the New Testament* (New York: Scribner's, 1956), p. 3.

Across America, piety and politics collided noisily.[9] Liberal churchmen applauded the Warren Court, conservative churchmen ignored or deplored it; ultra-conservative churchmen attacked it; "Impeach Earl Warren" billboards appeared in the American South and Southwest. Some church members, supporting the political rightists, called for Chief Justice Warren's impeachment and defamed liberal legislators. Next, the nomination and election of Catholic John Kennedy added heat to the church-state issue. But, there was more: the civil rights struggle, the poverty campaign, the Vietnam War, campus unrest, and the ABM controversy exploded the "politics-piety issue" into every American hamlet during the 1960s.

A Presbyterian minister, Eugene Carson Blake, now the retired executive secretary of the World Council of Churches, and at that time, the chief executive officer of his denominational church, was jailed in Baltimore for his part in a civil rights demonstration in Baltimore (1963). A Unitarian minister, James Reeb, was clubbed to death in the "national" civil rights demonstrations in Mississippi (1963). A Baptist minister, Martin Luther King, Jr., was shot to death in Memphis (1968). A middle-aged *religious* pacifist and Yale graduate, David Dellinger, was one of the "Chicago Seven" (1970). A Roman Catholic priest, Daniel Berrigan, who had been convicted for rifling selective service records in Catonsville, Maryland, and was a fugitive from the law, was captured by the FBI in August, 1970, at the Block Island home of William Stringfellow, Episcopal lay theologian, and poet Anthony Towne, both of whom were at odds

---

[9] See Erling Jorstad, *The Politics of Doomsday: Fundamentalists of the Far Right* (Nashville: Abingdon Press, 1970).

with the state. His brother, Philip Berrigan, and a nun, Elizabeth McAllister, were, along with five others, tried in the Federal District Court in Harrisburg, Pennsylvania, for subversion in 1972, and acquitted on that charge. The collisions between state and church were resounding through the corridors of daily life in America during the 1960s.

Conservative churchmen, too, were caught up in and contributed to the furore stirred by politics and piety. The late Reinhold Niebuhr and Carl McIntire, poles apart theologically and politically, attacked the "house religion" on the Potomac. Meantime, the International Congress on Evangelism, meeting in Minneapolis in 1969, demonstrated the willingness of conservative churchmen, led by Dr. Graham's brother-in-law and co-evangelist, Leighton Ford, to relate their evangelistic efforts to social issues. Not only liberal but moderate and conservative churchmen have gotten involved in political issues since the 1950s. The religious-political situation in the United States is presently ambiguous, divisive, explosive.[10]

Millions of churchmen, lay and clerical, are now convinced that active involvement in politics is a vindication of true piety. Others, like Paul Ramsey, Helmut Thielicke, and Will D. Campbell, are more cautious about the church's involvement. Professor Thielicke, for example, argues for the liberation of the commands and promises of God from a false restriction "to a purely personal and private arena" and urges a shift to the church's active recognition of God's "claim upon public life as well."

[10] See Fisher, *Politics, Poker, and Piety,* chapters 1 and 4 for a more extensive presentation.

He is persuaded, however, that "the church cannot do this by advancing political and social programs. What it must do is to show men whose consciences are bound by the Word of God that the divine commands have particular relevance also to the substantive decisions they make." [11]

But these men are not suggesting that Christianity has no relationship with political decisions. The church in the 1970s will be increasingly involved in politics (positively and negatively) as the citizens of this nation wrestle with military budgets, economic aid to Vietnam, amnesty, bureaucratic government, corporate and personal welfare, federal aid to private schools, abortion, nuclear armaments, ecological reforms, foreign aid, etc. Evangelism, social ministry, and social action will be fused more widely in Christian thought and action.

The outcome of the church's witness, or lack of it, is hidden from us. The church may suffer persecution. It may have a diminishing influence in public life. On the other hand, the church reborn could be the means God uses to renew human society. "We [churchmen] need to believe in the depths of our souls that God is greater than all the aggregations of human power, that the life of the spirit is more real than the technical mastery of things, that love is stronger in the end of the day than force. What matters is not the assertion of this truth in words, but living by that faith in the confidence that God will not disappoint or betray those who trust in Him." [12]

[11] Helmut Thielicke, *Theological Ethics: Vol. II, Politics,* p. 648.

[12] *Man's Disorder and God's Design,* the Amsterdam Assembly Series, (New York: Harper, 1948), Vol. III, chapter 12, "And Now?" by Emil Brunner, p. 180.

Chapter 5, a survey of organization and procedures for "doing" evangelism, suggests how some churches go about this essential work. Although each congregation must develop programs that "work" in its own situation, the knowledge of what other churches do may be helpful.

V
Getting It on the Road

During the 1950s, uncritical Protestant congregations accepted slick evangelism programs concocted in the central offices of their several denominations. There was great activity, and there *was* numerical growth. But it is likely that that growth and the church building boom—given the ebullient mood of the 1950s—would have occurred without the "don't-miss-a-step" programs of evangelism. A superficial religious revival was sweeping the country. Even in those now culturally distant years a few congregations balked at "program evangelism" on principle and questioned the "revival" itself. The maverick congregations were suspect in church circles, for in those years the "organization man" controlled ecclesia even as he controlled business, government, and public education. Conformity was the life-style; its shaky foundation, soon to crumble, was consensus thinking.

The climate in the 1970s is radically different. Key 73 encouraged each denomination and sect—and each congregation—to do its own thing evangelistically, to find its own way programatically, to fashion its own style of witness. But if, as Halford Luccock once observed, a sermon can splatter gelatinously around the walls of the sanctuary for want of a skeletal outline, so too can the

spirit of evangelism be dissipated and the content of
evangelism be atomized for want of effective institutional
forms. Consequently, several observations on how some
congregations do evangelism may be suggestive, corrective,
or supportive in getting evangelistic work underway in
one's own congregation.

Rarely does any parish start from scratch; evangelism
is *already* underway in most congregations. Wherever
Christians assemble to worship God, corporate and personal witness is being made. Wherever forty or eighty, or
two or three hundred, or two or three thousand persons
congregate, receive the Word of God in preaching, teaching, and sacraments—and go out to do the Word—there
is Christian witness. Every congregation's disciplined response in worship is corporate witness; and that corporate
witness depends on personal witness. When a family arises
each Sunday morning and attends a particular church, that
family makes a witness in their community. They are
telling their neighbors that Jesus Christ is more important
to them than Dagwood Bumstead, Lil' Abner, Peanuts,
the latest story about "Broadway Joe" Namath, extra
sleep, golf, etc. Given human nature, there are some pretenders (hypocrites) in every Christian congregation. But
most people who attend church regularly are not only
acknowledging publicly that they need the Christian God
but also that they want to live more responsibly in society,
and many do. Wherever the Word of God is preached and
taught in an assembly which meets voluntarily to hear that
Word and act on it, however falteringly, at home, at work,
and in the community, evangelism is underway.

Wherever congregations receive material gifts, presented voluntarily and specifically to carry on Christ's

ministry, evangelism is underway. The mature congregation is concerned, of course, that these gifts will be used to bring Christ's ministry to as many people in as many places, and as effectively, as possible. Consequently, responsible congregational leaders examine periodically the effectiveness of their church's ministry and seek to improve and enlarge it. An alert, honest leadership will face hard realities. Some church buildings *are* too costly to maintain; the decision to close them is made. Some professionals *are* ineffective in particular situations; the decision to help them serve another parish is made. Some congregations *are* so ingrown, so hopelessly mired down in dead tradition, that Christianity's prophetic voice is irretrievably stilled; the decision to release the members to other congregations or merge with another congregation is made.

Most congregations, however, deserve not less money but more to broaden and deepen their ministries. Where that kind of support is given—and it is to the tune of 9.1 billions of dollars each year—evangelism is underway. Wherever a congregation pays salaries to competent full-time staff members evangelism is underway, because these professionals seek out individuals and families in the community, present the cause of Christ to them, and persuade some to join his church. More significantly, these paid professionals search out and train ten or twenty (in a few churches, several hundred) laymen who acknowledge, accept, and act on Jesus' directive to witness person-to-person in the world. A congregation's economic investment in competent leadership pays dividends in a multiple witness, clerical and lay.

Wherever a congregation—by prophetic proclamations from its pulpit, formal statements from its official board, or by petitions from its people—expresses itself plainly on a particular social or political issue in the light of God's Word, evangelism is being implemented. Wherever a congregation serves economically depressed persons at home and abroad, evangelism is underway. Secular society may not appreciate what that particular congregation is saying or working for (some Christians will differ with them, too), but that is not at issue here. The point is that wherever the church works for a just society and serves persons, evangelism is underway. The Word joined with the concerned deed is Christian witness.

It is necessary, of course, to motivate members to do person-to-person evangelism, to teach them the content of evangelism, and to equip them with skills for evangelistic work. Naturally, different denominations seek to accomplish this task in different ways. Indeed, different congregations in the same denomination in the same city go about it in different ways. Some practices, methods, and procedures, however, are fairly common among the Christian churches.

Generally, the congregation has a standing Committee on Evangelism under the direction of the official board. On the other hand, some congregations are more highly organized. They have a Committee for Outreach, a Committee for Inreach, and a Committee to Integrate New Recruits during their first year. For most churchmen this is too much machinery; they opt for a single Committee on Evangelism which incorporates all three responsibilities. Usually, but not always, the Committee on Evangelism is chaired by a member of the official board and staffed by members from the board and the congregation; the latter represent different organizations, interests, and age groups in the church. It is the explicit responsibility of the Committee on Evangelism to oversee and direct the evangelistic work of the congregation. The professionals (clergy) also evangelize, but their primary responsibility is to motivate and equip the congregation to evangelize.

A few congregations use four separate standing committees to oversee and direct evangelistic work: (a) for the congregation, (b) for the church school, (c) for the youth group, and (d) for the auxiliaries of the congregation. But this pattern also calls for more machinery than most churchmen want to administer. A sound rule of thumb is to study one's own situation and adapt or devise a flexible structure and program that *works* in one's own congregation. In this present era of rapid social change, a responsible official board and its Evangelism Committee scrutinize periodically a program that is working effectively so that necessary changes can be effected before the need for them becomes critical. Toward this end, some official boards ask their standing committees on evangelism, social action, social ministry, and parish education to meet jointly at least once a year.

Many congregations have an organized group of lay evangelists who function under the oversight of the Committee on Evangelism. Depending on the maturity and vitality of the church, the number of these evangelists varies from a few to hundreds. One center-city church with sixteen hundred communing members has five hundred persons—a third of the membership—involved organizationally in its evangelistic work. Two hundred of these (one hundred couples) do the person-to-person visitation.

They meet regularly as the Order of St. Andrew. Other congregations have similar groups: the Fishermen's Club, the Seventy, the Ambassadors, the Witnesses, etc.

Ideally, every member of the official board should be an active evangelist. But that is not the case in most congregations. Consequently, some clergy are convinced that new life in the parish—edification and evangelism in the church—must begin at the top; the members of the official board must be converted or replaced by converted Christians. That is one of the theses we applied in an urban congregation and described in my report on parish renewal, titled *From Tradition to Mission*. In 1952, only two members of the twenty-one–member Vestry at Trinity Church were active evangelists; the other nineteen viewed evangelism as an elective. Since 1958, all twenty-one persons have been active evangelists; some are strikingly effective. For more than a decade one of the four qualifications for nomination for Trinity's official board is that each person nominated shall be a practicing evangelist.[1] Trinity's official board also visits, for example, the peripheral members to discuss Christ's claim on them. These are not easy visits; neighbor confronts neighbor on the responsibilities of churchmanship.[2]

It is not necessary for every board member to be knowledgeable about church accounts or investments. It is not necessary for every board member to examine the specifications for a new boiler. It is not necessary for every board member to be a church school teacher to

[1] See Fisher, *From Tradition to Mission,* pp. 68-81.

[2] *Ibid.,* chapter 5. See also Trinity's Membership Policy on membership responsibilities, Appendix I, pp. 119-125.

appreciate the need for solid parish education.[3] But it *is* essential that every board member be an active evangelist. Indeed, it is the responsibility of every church member to say a good word for Jesus. The first step toward that goal is to require it in fact of every nominee for the official board.

Ideally, all members in all congregations should be evangelists. Except for the Mormons and Jehovah's Witnesses, that is not the pattern in Protestant and Catholic churches. Consequently, to do person-to-person evangelism in any congregation, it is first necessary to recognize that few members engage in it. Next, it is necessary to recruit from the congregation ten or twenty or fifty or several hundred people to be motivated for and trained in that work. It is imperative to keep at this task year after year.

In addition to the *continuing* need to recruit, train, *and retrain* lay evangelists it is equally needful to encourage them in the systematic study of the scriptures, daily prayer, and direct involvement in persuading particular persons to accept church membership. It is, of course, the responsibility of the clerical and lay leaders of the congregation to help all the members to engage in Bible study, to pray for particular persons by name and need, to provide the names of persons for visitation, and to witness daily in word and deed.

Obtaining the names of unchurched persons is a tedious but essential task that each Evangelism Committee must work out for itself. The logistics for this mun-

[3] However, 90 percent of Trinity's vestry are serving presently or have served as teachers in the church school. *Ibid.,* chapter 4.

dane aspect of evangelism depend on congregational vitality and integrity, population of the community, location of the church, and the residence and profile of the membership. Some congregations are so vital that scores of members provide a steady flow of prospect cards for the lay evangelists to work from.

The organizational program for lay visitation varies from congregation to congregation. It also changes over the years in the same congregation. During the last two decades in Trinity Church we first employed a loosely knit organization of evangelists called the Seventy. Their work was directed by a Vestry Committee on Evangelism and the senior pastor. Next, we engaged in program evangelism. It failed in our situation, although it has been and is effective in other congregations, especially in the South. We followed our programmatic failure with the then widely used under-shepherding plan: the congregation was districted; each team of under-shepherds accepted responsponsibility for (a) a half dozen parish families, (b) for providing prospect cards, and (c) for visiting prospective members in their geographic area.

At present, we have returned to the more flexible style of evangelism that we used effectively in the late 1950s and early 1960s. Its basic thrust depends on a hundred couples (two hundred presons)—the Order of St. Andrew—who meet periodically for instruction and shared experiences. This group—comprised of experienced and inexperienced evangelists—was invited recently to a new series of training sessions, the eleventh series in twenty-one years.[4] One hundred and eighty-eight persons responded to this invitation *and* participated in the sessions. Another thirty-two persons later accepted a place in the Order of St. Andrew (220 persons). The Order meets at least two times a year to dig into the Faith and to discuss their evangelistic work. Absentees (illness or business demands) call at the office for tapes of each session missed.

Second, we have gathered another group of three hundred persons called Christ's Deputies. The name was defined simply: a deputy is one who acts in behalf of his chief (deputy secretary general, deputy sheriff). Christ's Deputies act for him; they accept his authority. The Deputies make personal evangelism calls only if they are motivated to do so. Their primary task is to keep alert in their personal relationships to discover persons who are unchurched in the community. The Deputies submit the names of these persons—and brief biographies—to the Evangelism Committee. This bloc of names is the primary source for evangelistic visits, but it is not the only source for visitation assignments. The congregation and visitors provide a solid secondary source.

Patterns of evangelistic visitation vary from congregation to congregation. Some congregations (as described above) manage to motivate their lay evangelists so that evangelistic work (person-to-person) is going on every day. Most congregations, it appears, concentrate their lay visitations in two, three, or four seasons of the year. Each congregation must decide for itself whether seasonal visitation is adequate. Some congregations designate one evening each week or month for visitation. More and more congregations are assembling a corps of visitors periodically for fellowship, the assignment of visitation cards, and visits that same evening with a "report back" before

10:00 p.m. Others employ this procedure only in Lent and/or Advent. A few, usually those with a staff ministry, keep person-to-person visits going every day of the year.

But there is no "best way" to evangelize except the way that *works* (the reader will recall the context of the first four chapters) in one's own congregation. But it is not likely that any "way" will work unless a corps of lay evangelists is recruited, instructed, motivated, guided, and encouraged to do evangelistic work.

Another elemental strand in effective evangelism is an edifying and meaningful study class for new members. Again, there is no best way to persuade and edify prospective members to take responsible places in Christ's church. The kinds of classes vary from denomination to denomination. Some congregations—The Church of the Saviour in Washington, D.C.—rely not only on an extended period of instruction but also on a season of *probationary* membership. Most main-line Protestant congregations, however, are less demanding; they conduct two to nine series of classes each year, the number of weekly sessions in each series ranging from two to eight. In our peripatetic society, it is already needful in metropolitan areas to provide *two* weekly opportunities per class session: Sunday morning during the church school hour and a stated week night. The prospective attends either at his convenience.

The content as well as the format of the classes varies between and among churches. Whatever number of meetings may be required, and whatever content is offered, responsible instruction for membership in any congregation will include (a) an honest presentation on how that particular congregation understands and interprets the scriptures; (b) a forthright description of the style and expectations of the congregation; (c) a candid presentation on those church doctrines that are held firmly, those that are held loosely, and those that are ignored; (d) a factual statement on the congregation's involvement with social, economic, and political issues.[5] Laity as well as clergy share the teaching responsibilities in each series of classes.

The other substantial source of new members for Christian churches is the young people between thirteen and fifteen years of age—the "baptized" roll.[6] Instruction periods for these teen-agers vary strikingly: from six weeks to three years. These classes (the confirmation class, the communicants' class, etc.) provide the Protestant and Catholic churches with a steady flow of new members. The content in the class courses should reflect firmly the theological foundations of each "tradition"; the style and expectations will reflect, consciously or unconsciously, the nature and character of the particular congregation. Tragically, the teaching in many of these classes is superficial, mechanical, dull. This, linked with the fact that many churches fail to provide continuing Christian instruction for middle and late teen-agers that is relevant to their daily lives, contributes to the church's awesome loss of young members between the ages of fourteen and twenty-one years.

Finally, each congregation must *care* for all its new

[5] See Gabriel Fackre, *Do and Tell: Engagement Evangelism in the '70s* (Grand Rapids: Eerdmans, 1973). An excellent handbook for lay evangelists, especially chapters 3, 4, and 5.

[6] The Baptists are the main exception here, but the children of their adult members provide a similar source of members.

members. Except in numerically small congregations in which the minister and several laymen can shepherd each new member, it is necessary to fashion a structured approach for the specific care of new members until they are "at home" in the congregation and, like older members, come under general pastoral care. A variety of ways are employed by different congregations, but many churchmen, taking their cue from professional football's "one-on-one defense," simply assign mature members (adults and teens) to look after new members for a full year. From the first day on, however, the effective care of church members reflects the integrity of the whole congregation.

o   o   o

The effective evangelist studies the scriptures to hear God speak. He prays for his candidate(s) for the kingdom. He witnesses person-to-person, seeking to persuade some persons in their freedom to decide for Christ and his church. The evangelist is most effective when he remembers that it is the Treasure which liberates persons, *and* that the Treasure requires earthen vessels to get into the world (Bible, sacraments, and *persons* preaching and teaching and witnessing and serving). Like the Apostle Paul, the Christian evangelist in our technological-nuclear society can also claim: "Christ is appealing through me." From the beginnings of the church, that has been and continues to be the dynamic reason for and the pervasive power in Christian evangelism.

Because we have Good News, we evangelize!

Appendix I
Membership Policy

Trinity Lutheran Church
31 South Duke Street
Lancaster, Pennsylvania

At the June, 1969, Vestry meeting, Dr. Fisher appointed, among other committees, a committee on membership to study the current membership policy in force in Trinity Church, affirm it, recommend changes in it, or fashion a new policy. Chairman Wilfred P. Bennett and his fellow-members—A. Reynolds Coulson, William J. Deisley, Robert P. Desch, Melvin J. Evans, Nancy L. Neff, James L. Rhoads, Robert H. Witmer, M. D.—met first on 20 July, 1969. After a series of meetings, reported periodically in Vestry, the Membership Committee submitted a new policy statement for study and review at the regular meeting of Vestry on 1 December, 1969. The Vestry—following a two-hour, section-by-section review and amendment of the document—endorsed it unanimously and placed it in effect, 1 January, 1970. This policy statement by the elected lay representatives of the Lutheran Church of the Holy Trinity reflects the biblical preaching-teaching-serving ministry of the congregation.

The Vestry recognizes the need to administer the policy flexibly, particularly with those who are physically and situationally limited in their possible involvement in worship and witness in and through Trinity Church (shut-ins, college students, military personnel). The policy is positive; it aims primarily to see that persons are shepherded in a meaningful relationship with Christ and other persons.

For the Vestry,
Melvin J. Evans, Secy.

I. Church Membership.—Membership in the church means that we have accepted God's invitation to become his people, to respond affirmatively to his saving act in Jesus Christ. This invitation is open to all, but no one is forced to accept it against his will. However, once a person freely accepts the responsibilities of church membership, he places his life under the authority of Christ, and other loyalties take second place. More and more he bases his actions on his response to that authority, for example:

1. Worshiping regularly in the company of those who have assembled in Christ's name to expose themselves to the healing Word of God in the words of men.

2. Encouraging others to hear the Word of God in preaching and teaching and to accept the new life which is offered in Jesus Christ.

3. Participating in the sacrament of Holy Communion.

4. Giving in a self-disciplined manner as he seeks to serve the Lord with gladness in the use of his ability, time, and possessions.

5. Being a neighbor, as Jesus defined the word, to those persons in need of a neighbor, regardless of where they live or who they are.

6. Praying, praising God for his blessings, and interceding for friends and enemies alike.

7. Working for honest, open, and loving relationships with parents, husband or wife, and children, since all aspects of family life are Christian vocation.

In a Christian person or in a Christian congregation, these are some of the signs of an inner change that allows us to look at life differently from the way we did before. But these are not accomplishments that we claim as our own. They are the fruits of our saying "yes" to God so that we become his agents in our time and place. Since God refuses to condemn us for our failures, can we take credit for our achievements? Rather, we say, "not on my own, but by the grace of God."

II. Church Discipline Regarding Membership, Marriage, Baptism and Burial.—One becomes a member of the church through participation in a particular Christian congregation or Christian community. The leaders of the congregation will show concern for all members. They recognize that persons differ in their capacities for participating in the church's witness and that individuals move at different paces in their growth toward Christian maturity. At the same time, the leadership, within its own human limitations, cannot ignore the responsibility of keeping the church true to its mission. The Vestry of the Lutheran Church of the Holy Trinity accepts the responsibility of helping members in their Christian growth and of confronting those who refuse to be concerned about it—that is, those who have really taken the Lord's name in vain. As a matter of integrity and with God's help, we cannot allow persons to use the church for their own ends (for example: as a baptizing, marrying, and burying association where one pays dues for services received —services which often provide nothing more important than cultural respectability). Such churchmanship is sham when compared with Jesus' declaration that if one is really serious about associating with him, he had better accept his particular cross and get on with it.

   A. *Membership*. Any member who within the limits of his ability does not willingly accept the disciplines inherent in biblical faith (for example: worshiping steadily, receiving the Lord's Supper, practicing responsible stewardship, and serving his neighbor) has by his own indifference and in his own freedom removed himself from active membership, as defined by this policy statement, in the Lutheran Church of the Holy Trinity. Such a person may, by Vestry action acknowledging that decision, no longer be carried on the membership roll of Trinity Church.

While none of us perfectly fulfills God's expectations with respect to his church, it is essential that minimum standards be used by the leadership for defining continued membership in the Lutheran Church of the Holy Trinity. Failure to meet these minimal standards indicates to the Vestry that one has terminated his own membership:

1. Attendance at a stated worship service at least once each month.

2. Participation in Holy Communion at least once a year.

3. Growing involvement in the ministry of the church with both service and money.

The third statement is difficult to apply, and each member is asked to discipline himself in this respect. However, flagrant inconsistencies between a member's stewardship (time, talent, money) and his standard of living, for example, will be one basis for Vestry action. Membership is reclaimed by attendance at a series of membership classes, through a pastoral conversation, and by reaffimation of faith.

Furthermore, a member who, despite counseling, persists vigorously in public declarations or actions that deny the authority of Jesus Christ, opens himself to excommunication. Excommunication removes a person from the membership roll of Trinity Church. Such action, of course, is based on human judgment, subject to human limitations, and must never be confused with God's final judgment of that person. Rather, excommunication is a temporary disciplinary measure, anticipating the return of that person in faith and openness to the church community.

B. *Marriage*. Before performing the marriage ceremony, the pastor, through counseling with the persons about to be married, shall be satisfied that the contemplated union is in keeping with the Word of God and in accordance with the laws of the Commonwealth. No marriage shall be performed unless the counseling pastor is convinced that God's blessing may properly be asked upon it.

At least one of the persons to be married shall be a member, as defined by this policy statement, of the Lutheran Church of the Holy Trinity.

All arrangements for the marriage service, music, and the use of facilities—and the pre-marriage counseling itself—shall be made in consultation with one of the pastors of Trinity Church, who shall be the officiant for the marriage service.

It would be hypocritical to ask God's blessing on a couple in marriage unless both accept as a Christian vocation of the highest calling their relationships with each other, their families, and the children who may be born to them.

C. *Baptism*. Only members of a Christian congregation shall be accepted as sponsors of children for Baptism. Prior to the Baptism, parents and sponsors must be pastorally instructed in their spiritual responsibility to the child.

It would be dishonest for any person, parent or sponsor, who presents a child for Baptism to participate in this Christian sacrament while rejecting the claims of Christian vocation inherent in child-rearing and family life.

Likewise, it would be hypocritical for the church to confer Christian Baptism on any adult who rejects being counted as a member of the church.

D. *Burial*. In the event of the death of a member, the pastor who is serving shall advise the family of the availability of the Sanctuary or the Rengier Chapel. Neither the Sanctuary nor the Chapel shall be used for anyone who is not a member, as defined by this policy statement, of the Lutheran Church of the Holy Trinity at the time of death.

It would not only be hypocrisy but also a violation of human freedom to provide a Christian burial service for one who rejected or ignored during his life the claims of the church. But again, it is important that human judgments about a person not be mistaken for God's final judgment of him. In cases where Christian burial does not openly violate the freedom of the deceased person, a Christian burial service can be provided whenever it seems appropriate. However, such an act does not confer after death an implied membership in the Lutheran Church of the Holy Trinity which did not in fact exist at the time of death.

Exceptions to any of these policies, under unique and unusual circumstances, shall be made by the Pastor in consultation with the Executive Committee of the Vestry.

When we accept Christ's authority as individuals who find unity with him and one another through the church, we willingly and gladly accept disciplines and responsibilities that reshape our lives. At the same time, we receive gifts that allow us to become more nearly the persons God intended—

less selfish, more compassionate
less guilt-ridden, more healthy-minded

    less dishonest, more authentic
    less the victims of our culture, more nearly free
    less concerned with the death of the body, more con-
       cerned with passing from death into life, beginning
       here and now.

Appendix II
The Call
(To Lay Teachers in the Church School)

This call to teach in the _____ Department of the _____ Church School of the Lutheran Church of the Holy Trinity is hereby extended to you after careful consideration and earnest prayer.

This call is extended to you in full confidence:
1. That you are committed to the Person of Jesus Christ, our Lord.
2. That you share the basic confessional position of the Lutheran Church, as enunciated in the Augsburg Confession and Luther's Small Catechism, copies being attached hereto.
3. That you worship regularly within the fellowship of Trinity Lutheran Church.
4. That you are an increasingly responsible steward of your possessions, either accepting in reality or as your goal the tithe as the first reasonable step in Christian giving.
5. That you will earnestly consider, against your own background, training, experience, and felt needs, the worth of opportunities offered for further training.
6. That you believe in and act upon the prior call of every Christian to the task of personal evangelism.
7. That you will conscientiously strive to nurture in Christian growth those placed under your care, making use of all resources available and taking as your own the responsibility to hold them by prayer and visitation.

It is expected that you will pray earnestly as you consider this call, remembering not only that he who teaches is judged with great strictness but also that from those to whom much has been given much is expected.

In Christian Witness Whereto
We Here Affix Our Signatures:

_____

Superintendent

_____

Department Superintendent

Acceptance

Mindful of the sacred trust to those who teach the gospel of Jesus Christ our Lord, and of the joy which comes to those who serve him, I hereby accept this call extended in the name of the Church School Association of the Lutheran Church of the Holy Trinity, Lancaster, Pennsylvania, to teach in the _____ Department of the School or to serve as _____ of the school.

Signed _____

Appendix III
Letter to Evangelists

Dear Co-worker with Christ:

Evangelism is one firm thrust in Trinity's corporate ministry in 1973. You are among 200 persons called to join the core group of lay evangelists. You will be spokesmen for Authentic Living. You will reclaim a distinguished name in Trinity's recent history—the Order of St. Andrew.

The group's main purpose is evangelism—inreach (lapsed members) and outreach (new members). Your work will receive the full support of the entire staff. You will receive regular support (call assignments, counsel, guidance) from the pastoral office.

You will be equipped initially for this ministry in three training sessions in the Fondersmith Auditorium. Nursery care will be provided. Each of the following presentations will run thirty minutes with thirty minutes for questions and discussion.

Monday, 12 February - 7:30 P.M.
Evangelism—Biblical Foundations and Expectations
Pastor Evelan

Monday, 19 February - 7:30 P.M.
Evangelism—Theological Foundations and Expectations
Pastor Lehman

Monday, 26 February - 7:30 P.M.
Evangelism—Existential Foundations and Expectations
Doctor Fisher

We challenge you in Christ's Name to accept this call by attending the training sessions and engaging quickly—that is, without any delay—in person-to-person evangelism.

Faithfully, your pastors,